Cara Meredith's storytelling offers moments of revelation that humanize our society's struggles with racial division while pointing toward hope for overcoming our divides. Don't be surprised to find yourself stretched and transformed by her prophetic message.

—*Edward Gilbreath,* author, *Reconciliation Blues* and *Birmingham Revolution*

This candid, thoughtful memoir of Cara's exploration of racial identity teaches us, but it does so through an invitation into Cara's thoughts and fears, bumbling mistakes and earnest reflections, and journey of discovering herself and her history. I am so grateful for the gift of this book.

—*Amy Julia Becker,* author, *White Picket Fences: Turning toward Love in a World Divided by Privilege*

Cara Meredith's journey is a challenging reminder that the road to racial justice begins with the tender first step of seeing the face of God in every soul looking back at us, including the face in the mirror.

—*Patricia Raybon,* author, *My First White Friend: Confessions on Race, Love, and Forgiveness*

Cara honors the stories and experiences of her father-in-law, her husband, and the greater black community as she traces her narrative and discusses the challenges of her journey. This book is a moving and insightful resource for all of us.

—*Ken Wytsma,* lead pastor, Village Church; author, *The Myth of Equality*

Cara blends personal insights, thoughtful research, helpful lessons, and hope on this emotionally charged subject. Draw close, listen, learn, be challenged and encouraged, and take the next step toward love and justice.

—*Vivian Mabuni,* speaker; author, *Warrior in Pink* and *Open Hands, Willing Heart*

This book advises like a trusted friend, making it an essential contribution to the conversation on racial reconciliation. This book is reshaping my understanding of the *imago Dei,* inviting me to see more clearly the vibrant beauty and rich opportunities of diversity.

—*Jer Swigart,* cofounding director, Global Immersion Project; coauthor, *Mending the Divides*

This book is a gift especially to white people like me who are confronting our blindness and pleading for our sight to be healed. Cara's winsome, personal, and captivating storytelling helps pull back our cultural blinders so we can see in full color, leading to redemption for all of us.

—*Jon Huckins,* cofounding director, Global Immersion Project; coauthor, *Mending the Divides*

Cara has written a beautiful, rich accounting of the power of love to bridge the divisions we establish between one another. This memoir is a powerful gift for those who seek hope and healing in a divided world.

—*Deidra Riggs,* author, speaker, disco lover

Cara has given us a way to posture our hearts and minds toward personal and interpersonal considerations of race while holding systemic-cultural considerations firmly in mind. This is a fascinating, challenging, and encouraging record of lived knowledge and practiced wisdom.

—*Justin McRoberts,* author, *Prayer: Forty Days of Practice*

Cara takes us on her journey of stepping out of her protective bubble and running headlong into reality. From the moment I picked this book up, I couldn't put it down. I trust you'll have the same experience.

—*Marlena Graves,* author, *A Beautiful Disaster: Finding Hope in the Midst of Brokenness*

In a world where many folks want to be colorblind, Cara invites us to see the world in full color and declare that every person is as beautiful as God is. She dares us to dream of the world as it should be, inviting us to join her in the streets as we build that world.

—*Shane Claiborne,* author and activist; cofounder, The Simple Way and Red Letter Christians

Cara invites us to join her in a space where the systems that separate us are seen, acknowledged, and reckoned with. Her words are necessary especially for white folks like myself who need help confronting our privilege and finding our way toward justice and reconciliation.

—*Micha Boyett,* author, *Found: A Story of Questions, Grace, and Everyday Prayer*

the Color of Life

A JOURNEY TOWARD LOVE AND RACIAL JUSTICE

Cara Meredith

ZONDERVAN

ZONDERVAN

The Color of Life
Copyright © 2019 by Cara Meredith

Requests for information should be addressed to:
Zondervan, *3900 Sparks Dr. SE, Grand Rapids, Michigan 49546*

ISBN 978-0-310-35184-9 (softcover)

ISBN 978-0-310-35774-2 (audio)

ISBN 978-0-310-35300-3 (ebook)

To James, Canon, and Theodore,
the three who hold my heart

Lana,
to the conversation!

[signature]

Contents

Foreword by James Howard Meredith 9

Introduction 11

1. Beginnings 15
2. More to the Story 21
3. Seeing Color for the First Time. Again. 26
4. Well, I Love You 34
5. Three Years in Mississippi 54
6. 1967, Then and Now 69
7. Differences 80
8. Black Santa 90
9. Learning to Listen 102
10. Little Caramels 114
11. *Imago Dei* 124
12. The Problem 136
13. Not Noticing 149
14. A Beautiful Both-And 162
15. We, Ours, Us 177
16. Lamentations 187
17. Tramp, Tramp, Tramping of Feet 199

Afterword by James Henry Meredith 211

Acknowledgments 213

Notes 217

Recommended Reading 235

Foreword by James Howard Meredith

Cara is the mother of my two youngest grandchildren. She now faces the reality of raising two nonwhite boys to manhood in America. The problem is generally referred to as the racial problem by the experts. To me, it has always been a simple question: Who in America enjoys the rights of full citizenship?

Sitting on my desk, where I do most of my work, is a picture of my father's mother, who lived the first twelve years of her life as a white woman. Her father had her reclassified from white to colored in 1875 for political reasons. She continued in his plantation school, later becoming the teacher at the school until the 1890s, but she was forbidden to teach her own children. What she did teach her children produced me. My grandmother used the Bible to lay a foundation for her downline, and she taught my father every book in the Bible, and my father taught me every book in the Bible by the time I was twelve.

Ole Miss, 1962. One week after I filed my application to attend Ole Miss, I wrote the Kennedy administration a letter. I asked one question: Am I a citizen or am I not a citizen? If I am a citizen, then I am entitled to all rights of American citizenship. Until Cara Meredith asked me to write about her book, I had never answered that question. I have now concluded that I, James Meredith, have enjoyed full first-class citizenship ever since American soldiers entered Mississippi that day in 1962, brought it again under federal control, occupied the university and the city of Oxford, and I walked into the Lyceum building, registered as a student, and walked across the campus and attended my first class. I have enjoyed my rights as a citizen since that time.

In 1966 I led The Meredith Walk Against Fear. It was much more important than one person's effort at Ole Miss. It touched the citizenship rights of every black person in Mississippi, in America, and around the world. I was wounded by a sniper on the second day. That act brought the question of who should enjoy the rights of citizenship to the American public. It brought the entire movement to Mississippi for three weeks under the leadership of Dr. Martin Luther King Jr. and James Meredith. We changed the wording of the event I was leading from "Walk" to "March" to accommodate the protest movement that Dr. King and others were leading. After all, a walk is the use of highways and byways to move from one place to another. A march is a protest against government policies used to keep some citizens from enjoying all rights of full citizenship, and a march is what we ended up doing.

My position was that there was no one big enough in America for me to protest against because the highest office in America is citizen. I believed then as I do now that I would have all rights of citizenship or die trying to get them.

Cara Meredith's book tells the story of where we were fifty-five years ago, where we are today, and where we need to go to make America right for all of her people, including my grandchildren.

—*James Howard Meredith, October 3, 2017*

Introduction

*W*e're white!" my three-year-old son yelled from the back seat before pausing to shout, "And blue!"

My husband, James, and I looked across the console to one another: *Did he just say what we think he said?* Eyebrows raised, we asked him to repeat himself.

"We're white!" Canon said again, more emphatically this time. "And blue! I already said that, Mama."

"I know, baby, I know," I replied, turning to face him, "but we're white and *black,* not white and blue." My fingers touched the skin of my other arm, and then my husband's, to the dark and light colors of his flesh and mine.

"Oh, yeah, black. Black, black, black." Canon repeated the information to himself, as if solidifying the colors of the rainbow in his head. Nodding, he turned toward the window, his mind already moving on to the next distraction, the next conversation. Our boy had begun to see color.

*I*f you were buried six feet underground, then you might be able to miss seeing color in the faces of this world. Subscribe to *National Geographic.* Turn on the evening news. Or better yet, take a walk in your neighborhood, your town, your city. Chances are, you're going to spot someone who doesn't look a whole lot like you, but someone who is just as human and just as divinely stamped as you. You're going to encounter another human who matters just as much as you matter.

In our house, we call this divine stamping the image of God, the belief that every human, everywhere, bears the resemblance of the Creator. You might call it *ubuntu,* a human-to-human honoring that happens because you and I are bound by our humanity. Or perhaps you call it the Buddha nature, believing the seed of enlightenment lives within every creature, from ant to hippopotamus to human beings. We tend to call it the *imago Dei,* the likeness of Christ made manifest, shaded in every color of the crayon box. From black and white and blue to tan and peach and purple, we see this image imprinted within its many hues, each variation an invitation to open our eyes and see holiness reflected back to us.

The homeless man sitting by the road begging for beer money? Christ made manifest. The grocery clerk standing on her feet all day saying a thousand hellos to a thousand different strangers? Christ made manifest. The nun walking through the subway station, the Buddhist monk catching the city bus, the window washer scrubbing the side of a Manhattan sky rise five hundred feet in the air? Christ made manifest, Christ made manifest, Christ made manifest. The image of God imprinted on every human, everywhere—the shiny stuff of heaven made tangible across the faces of ethnicities and cultures and people groups.

I have not arrived, for life is not a train ride with stops, the toot of a whistle signaling my finally reaching the place where I understand everything. But I have been on an adventure of learning to see the *imago Dei* in the faces around me, for this is a story of how love helped me see color and of how love helped me see God in the many faces of color. This is a story that looks at the pages of history alongside the pages on the internet. This is a story of the advantages that have been mine since our country's beginning. This is a story of anger and a story of sadness, a story of hope and a story of justice. But mostly, this is a story about two people who were unlikely to fall in love who also came to see what love for everyone is all about.

And this is an invitation from me to you to do the same. This is an invitation for you to *see*.

CHAPTER 1

Beginnings

Some couples meet at bars, while others find their lives intertwined on the first day of college. Some love stories rival the likes of *Casablanca,* and then some tales, like *Sleepless in Seattle,* involve backpack mishaps at the top of the Empire State Building, spurred on by a saddened boy's call to a radio show. James and I give all credit to Dr. Neil Clark Warren, creator of eHarmony.

I was thirty, he was forty-one. Both of us had been around the block, at least when it came to dating, to girlfriends and boyfriends, and to thinking we'd met The One when he or she wasn't actually our one. I had my dog, Mr. Darcy, but try as I might, all the *Pride and Prejudice* references in the world didn't proffer up a man to share life alongside. Unlike some of the other men I'd met, James held a steady job and lived on his own in a little pocket community outside of San Francisco. Plus, he knew the difference between *there, their,* and *they're,* had a book collection that extended beyond the likes of *The Left Behind* series, and seemed to spend a fair amount of time under Mother Nature's umbrella. By all outward appearances, he made the cut. After jumping through several rounds of companionability on the online dating site, we made it to the final round of open communication. "Email me," I wrote to him, certain he wouldn't. "Call me,"

I responded when his email arrived, certain he wouldn't. "Meet me?" I proposed, or maybe the question came from him. Within six weeks of our meeting virtually, we finally met flesh to flesh, sharing a bottle of pinot noir and a plate of Italian bruschetta at a wine bar on the corner of B Street and Vine.

He was already there when I arrived, a table set for two waiting for us. Minutes after we sat down, he pulled his iPhone out of his pocket, intensely focused on the screen before him. I glanced at the menu and looked across at him. My head shook in disbelief. Did he really value an email, a text message, or, God forbid, a Facebook status update more than the woman two feet in front of him? I closed my menu and began gathering my things.

"What are you doing?" James asked, looking up from the menu, a look of confusion spreading across his face.

Indignant that his devotion to an inanimate object wasn't much different from that of the sixteen-year-olds I worked with five days a week, I said, "I'm leaving! Obviously, whatever or whoever's on the other end of your cell phone is more important than me!"

An apologetic smirk spread across his mouth, his doe eyes steeped in laughter. "I was here a couple of weeks ago with some friends," he replied, turning his phone toward me. "We had this amazing bottle of wine. I took a picture of it and wanted to order it for the two of us tonight, but I just got this new phone and can't figure out how to scroll through my pictures any faster."

"Oh," I whispered, settling into the hardback chair. I wasn't going anywhere, at least not yet. So we talked about our vocations, about his work in the financial sector and mine in the nonprofit ministry world. We talked about traveling, how he wanted to visit a close friend from college who now lived in Israel, how I dreamed of spending two months holed up in a castle in Scotland, free to roam the emerald Highlands whenever I pleased. We talked about the border collie who held the keys to my heart, and about how he had never owned a pet.

"You've never had a pet, not even a frog or a cat or a hamster?"

"No pets."

"But you're willing to give one a try?" I asked him.

He smiled. "I'm willing to give Mr. Darcy a try," he replied, clinking his glass against mine for the ninth, tenth time that night. Conversation never waned and curiosity gripped me. We couldn't be more different from each other if we tried, but there was something about him, something that drew me to him, something that made me want to know more and hear more and learn more about his story.

Three hours later, he walked me to my car. We walked close to one another, bodies leaning into each other, fingertips touching, daring ourselves not to pull away, to stay for just a few seconds longer.

"I have to see you again," he said, pulling me toward him. I nodded my head. This would not be our last date if I had any say in the matter.

*J*ames was fourteen years old, a freshman at a private high school in Jackson, Mississippi. Not three years before, his mother, Mary June, a lifelong schoolteacher, had died unexpectedly of a heart attack. When she passed, his father knew that James and his twin brother, Joseph, could not get the best education possible if they stayed in Mississippi. Desiring the best for his sons and wanting to honor his wife's dreams for their educational development, he sent the twins away to boarding school in upstate New York for their seventh and eighth grade years.

After graduating from North Country School, James wanted to experience life on his own, finding his identity as an individual and not as part of an assumed pair. He moved back to Jackson for his ninth grade year, determined to live without apology in a place he hoped had changed for the better. But they still called him by the only name their mouths could utter.

"Boy!"

"Boy, watchchu doin' back here?"

"What's a black boy like you doin' thinkin' you can make somethin' of yourself in New York?"

Their voices were familiar echoes of hate. Within a couple of days, after they spit in his face and refused to call him by his given name, James realized how little things had changed in the great state of Mississippi—at least not for his white classmates who saw him only as a black boy. *If this is what life is going to be like for me in Mississippi,* he thought, *then I have to get out of here. I have to leave. I have to go where I am seen as a student who wants to obtain a quality education.* He trusted the words of his father, instilled deep within him: he could be and do anything he set his mind to, for he was not just a black boy who lived under a predetermined ceiling set by society.

Desperate to get away, he called Phillips Academy in Andover, Massachusetts, the boarding school he could have attended, where Joseph had already started his freshman year. *Too late,* the registrar replied. But if he could keep his grades up, he could enroll as a sophomore the next fall. So he did the only thing he could do: he focused on his studies and on achieving high grades. He tried his best to ignore their taunts and jeers.

I was fourteen years old, an eighth grader at Whiteaker Middle School in Keizer, Oregon. Some people said middle school is the hardest time of all: "You'll feel awkward," they said, all the changes in your body, all the different things that happen to you and make

you feel like you live in the Land of In-Between, where you are neither a kid nor a teenager. "You'll feel like you don't fit in," they said,
when you wonder who your friends are, when you can't seem to fit
in anywhere at all. But that hadn't been the case for me. When Mom
and Dad let me get contacts the summer after sixth grade, the scared
little girl hiding inside of me—the one they called Four Eyes, the
one they mockingly sang "Old MacDonald" to on the playground,
because the farmer and I shared the same last name—found she
wasn't so scared anymore.

It made me wonder whether the change was obvious to everyone
else when, at eighth grade graduation, I kept going up to the stage
to receive awards.

"Musician of the Year: Cara MacDonald." *Clap, clap, clap.*

"Community Service Student of the Year: Cara MacDonald."
Clap, clap, clap.

"Class award, voted Most Likely to be a Friend to Everyone:
Cara MacDonald." *Clap, clap, clap.*

I collected thirteen awards that night, from the National Honor
Society and the English teachers and even the principal too. Each
time I walked up the steps to the gymnasium's makeshift stage and
shook hands with the grown-up who handed me an award, I looked
out into the audience at my friends seated in the first couple of rows
and at my family, clumped together on the bleachers. My friends
yelled loudly, fingers to mouth, calling out nicknames and whistling
like their daddies taught them, hands clapping a thousand times a
minute. But the faces I most squinted to see were the four clumped
together on the bleachers: Dad, proud smile spread across the width
of his face, hands balanced on air, stilled in a shrug. "That's my girl!"
I imagined him shouting. Mom, who beamed from ear to ear, wiping
tears from her eyes between bursts of more clapping. And Brandon
and Aleah, my younger brother and sister, who nudged each other

with their elbows, giving high fives to everyone around them as they joined in the catcalls too.

If this was a taste of the life set before me, I had nothing to lose. *Bring it on,* I whispered, a three-word dare to my future and maybe even to the world. I could be and do anything I set my mind to because nothing was going to get in my way.

CHAPTER 2

More to the Story

*F*our days after our first date, James and I made plans to see one another again. Although I was moving earlier in the day, my mind swirled with the stuff romantic comedies are made of: sitting on the floor sharing pizza, unopened cardboard boxes decorating every corner of the room. When a handful of friends helped me move six miles south on the San Francisco Peninsula, from San Mateo to San Carlos, I told my friend Jenn a guy was coming over for a visit later that night.

"A guy?" She exclaimed. I could tell my words caught her by surprise.

"Yeah, a guy. You know, like a man, a suitor," I replied, giggling.

"Have you met this man before?" she asked, her jaw hanging open.

"We went out a couple of nights ago. But we've known each other since the beginning of September. We met online."

"Cara, are you kidding me? You're having a guy over to your apartment whom you met on the internet, whom you've seen in person one time? What if he's a dangerous criminal, a murderer, a rapist, a stalker?"

"He's not," I replied, pausing. "He's different. I really like him."

"Did you kiss him?"

"No, but when he kissed me, I gladly kissed him back." I did a little dance in my newly acquired living room, Mr. Darcy barking and jumping in excitement: *Play with me, play with me!* At the end of our conversation, Jenn and I made a deal: I promised to call her in the event of an emergency, acknowledging that James was still a stranger to me (albeit a most delectable stranger). In exchange, she would unpack some of the boxes in my new home so it would be presentable to a guest. I never did call her that evening, but I did send her a thank-you note. After all, her eye for welcoming a stranger into my home yielded me another kiss at the end of the evening, and yet another giddy schoolgirl dance when I closed the door behind him.

*L*ate the next afternoon, I drove sixteen miles north to the place where James lived. If I could host him five hours after moving every box of books and clothes and piece of secondhand furniture I owned, surely he could host me for an evening too. Soon enough, we settled into a simple dinner of pasta, salad, and the same pinot noir we'd shared on our first date. He moved through his place with ease, turning up the volume on the deep bass of a Marcus Miller album, gliding over hardwood floors his feet knew by heart. As my eyes followed his every move, my inner feminist seethed against my newly romantic self, upset by so quick a refutation of the values I'd long espoused. *Women don't need a man. A grown woman like myself can get by just fine on her own. Jerry Maguire doesn't have anything on me: I don't need someone to complete me.* But the more I stared at him, the more each bulletproof point failed to prove itself evincible.

Three dates in and I was nothing short of smitten. His speech, his actions, his mannerisms, all so different from my own, intrigued me. Captivated by our differences, I couldn't get enough of him. He was black, I was white. He was left brained, I was the epitome of right brained. He chewed his words softly, deliberately, sometimes passively; I spit sentences out of my mouth without a thought, too often asking forgiveness instead of permission. Eleven years my senior, he had graduated from the most elite high school in the United States, just as I was entering the second grade at a low- to average-performing public school. He said he liked to raise his hands when he worshiped God, maybe by culture, maybe by preference. I was drawn to candles and quiet chanting, prayers prayed round the world for thousands of years by thousands of tongues. Already I could tell he had a propensity for moodiness and melancholy, while I leaned toward optimism and sunshine, almost to a fault. On paper, we didn't stand a chance, but somehow our differences melded us in a way neither one of us could explain. We fit. We made sense. It was like the contrasting parts of our identities became our binding glue.

"There's something I want to show you," he said, interrupting my reverie. I turned to where he was standing in the living room, a number of books spread out on the coffee table before him. We sat down on the couch at the same time, cushions bursting upward, a shock of electricity shooting through my bones when our knees touched. What the man did to me with a mere bump of his leg! Flipping one of the photography books open, he turned to an ear-marked page of Martin Luther King Jr. standing alongside a handful of other African American men.

"This is my father," he said, pointing to a grainy black-and-white picture.

"Your dad is Martin Luther King?" I replied, incredulous.

"No, *this* is my dad," and he pointed to a man standing to King's right. King was immersed in conversation, lips pressed together, head leaning in closely to the man walking beside him whose fingers gripped a walking stick. A straw sun hat covered King's head, an African pith helmet topped the other man's head. Although sunglasses covered their eyes, the photographer captured a moment of intimacy between them, not unlike our own. I looked at the caption at the bottom of the picture: "Martin Luther King Jr. and James H. Meredith, March Against Fear, 1966."

"Um, who is he, James?" I whispered.

"His name is James Meredith, like me," he replied. "He was the first black man to graduate from the University of Mississippi in the early sixties."

I could feel him watching for a reaction as he said these words, waiting for my response, for who I'd be on the other side of the telling. Would I be like some of the women he'd dated who had wanted to be with him only because of his father's historical significance? Or would I swing like a pendulum to the other side and claim indifference, choosing not to fully understand the weight of his father's actions? The worst I could do was to leave his place later that night unchanged by the fragile piece of history that lived within his heart.

Shame about not knowing who his dad was washed over me, gulps of embarrassment sounding in my throat. I had probably heard of and studied James Meredith in my eighth and eleventh grade US history classes, just as I had likely read about him in college, especially in the education classes necessary for my teaching credential. But the information had gone in one ear and out the other, the advantages of not knowing and not remembering a luxury all my own. As a white person, it had been my luxury to remember crucial facts for a history exam because I deemed it the right thing to do, because we had to study and memorize the stories of significant African Americans every February during Black History Month. But now, as I sat beside a man whose father had left an indelible mark on the pages of history, I wondered what all I had missed, what all I hadn't learned, what all I hadn't committed to memory because it hadn't mattered enough for me to remember.

"This is huge, James. Your dad is a really big deal," I finally said. I flipped the pages of the books laid out before me: "James Meredith, escorted by US Marshals, on the way to registering for classes, 1962." *Flip.* "Jeering students wave the Confederate flag." *Flip.* "Two hundred people arrested in ensuing riots." *Flip.* "Kennedy sends 30,000 National Guard troops to Ole Miss." *Flip.* "James Baldwin and James H. Meredith, in front of a New York City brownstone." *Flip.* "James Meredith becomes the first African American to graduate from the University of Mississippi, 1963." The photographs blurred together, seemingly endless snapshots of an era so far from my comprehension. As James went on to explain, and as I saw in the pages that followed, his father's actions helped pave the way for equal opportunities and voting rights not only for African Americans but for every American citizen, of every skin color. One man's decision to integrate set the trajectory of his life and, as I soon learned, of his sons' lives too, garnering him status as a figurehead of the civil rights movement. This was the family, the father, and the legacy of the man sitting next to me, and I was utterly clueless to it all.

I could feel my heart pounding as history danced with the present moment, intermingling with possibilities of him and me and the life we might share. Had all of this not mattered to me because it hadn't affected me personally? Had I not cared about issues of race and justice and civil rights because I was white and he was black, because although this was a part of his history, I hadn't believed it a part of my history? Surely this hadn't been my fight to fight, my responsibility to bear.

But as I sat there on the couch next to a man whose differences I found irresistible, I wondered whether I'd gotten it all wrong. I wondered whether there might be more to the story than I'd been told, more to the story than the memories of my childhood held.

CHAPTER 3

Seeing Color for the First Time. Again.

*W*hen I was growing up, my family didn't fly a Confederate flag in our front yard, nor did we stretch one across the back of our burgundy and gold Ford Aerostar. I knew better than to yell the n-word on the playground—not at the majority of kids who looked mostly like me, and not at the handful of kids with darker skin. My parents put down roots in the Willamette Valley, a place that could give the lush hills of Ireland a run for its money, its land one of the richest soils in the United States. We boasted of hazelnuts and of every kind of berry growing wild alongside the Willamette River, a 187-mile tributary of the Columbia River. And since the Willamette was only a couple of blocks from our house, we called ourselves the luckiest people in the world to have landed there, to have dug into its soils.

One main road ran through our town, business lots bustling with fast-food joints, drive-thru coffee stands, and the occasional church. Clouds often dotted the sky, and an overcast gloom kissed the deep evergreens of backyard neighborhoods and mountainous horizons. The gray loomed so close you could almost touch it if you closed one eye and reached your finger toward the sky overhead. My life didn't revolve around my town or its beauty, though. My life revolved around my family.

Our home was one of food and faith, those elements the blocks in the foundation of our lives. We were salt of the earth kind of people: hardworking the bones of our bodies, good and honest the blood that pumped through our veins. We turned up the dial on the radio station when our favorite oldies song hit the airwaves, belting into wooden spoons the tunes we knew by heart. My siblings and I covered the living room in elaborate forts made of blankets and quilts held together by clothespins and masking tape. Under its shadow, we read books and played with our stuffed animals and drank warm mugs of hot cocoa, contentment ours for the keeping. And nearly every night, our family gathered around the table to share a meal.

"Cara, it's your turn," Mom would say, nodding at me.

"Again?"

"Cara, your turn," she would repeat, more emphatically this time, her eyes already closed. I had no choice in the matter.

"DearheavenlyFather,thankyouforthisfoodandforthisfamily, inyournameIpray,amen." Mom squeezed my hand, while Dad let out a Baptist's hearty "Amen!" Aleah and Brandon mumbled their so-be-it's too, before spinning the lazy Susan in a grab for all the taco fixings: ground beef, refried beans, tomatoes, lettuce, salsa, sour cream. We lifted tortilla shells from the warmer on the kitchen counter, greasy paper towels the only remaining evidence. We took seconds, thirds, filling our plates as much as we needed, as much as we wanted. Meanwhile, the national news droned on in the background, the television screen like a seventh member of the family, right after the bassett hound, Sir Hoover MacGruff.

"So, honey," Mom would ask, directing her question to each of her honeys at the table. "How was your day at school?"

"Fine," Aleah would mumble.

"Fine," Brandon would reply.

"Fine," I would say between bites, exasperated by her audacity to even ask my young adolescent self a question. No one could get in the way of my tacos, not even if hers were the hands that prepared it, hers the feet that stood in the hot kitchen dodging grease spit from the shells and meat we stuffed into our mouths.

"And honey, how was your day at work?" Dinner table conversation didn't tend to deviate much from day to day, at least from the mouth of babes, but my father was a different story.

*A*s a civil engineer, Dad was passionate about designing safety rails and concrete barriers for the state's highways and bridges. Eyes fixed to the television screen during dinnertime, he somehow managed to simultaneously devour his food, provide commentary on American politics, and update the family on his workday. "Can you even believe it?" he would exclaim between bites of refried beans. Like a set of bobblehead dolls, four heads would swivel to one side, gazing toward news of the Persian Gulf War or the latest presidential campaign, then back again. As soon as the news segment was over, Dad would begin to tell us about his day, his family a captive audience for his storytelling. He would tell us about driving to work with his coworker Gerry, their faces hidden behind plastic Groucho Marx glasses and fake mustaches in a ploy to put smiles on the faces of fellow commuters. He would also talk about the coworkers who could never understand the stress of his job, who didn't seem to get the pressure he was under. When taco bits flew across the table and his frustration mounted, sometimes our eyes shifted back to the television, its screen an escape from the rise of his emotions. Eventually, Dad bounced the question back to Mom, to her work as an instructional assistant at a local elementary school. She helped a little boy in the third grade read a book for the first time. She celebrated a retirement with the Learning Resource Center staff. She just could not get that *darn* costume sewn for the nativity pageant dress rehearsal. The highs and lows of their days became the highs and lows of our days too, the jobs they should have gotten and the accolades they should have received ours also to mourn and grieve.

But when it came to conversations of race, sometimes it felt like "Need Not Apply" had been stamped across our foreheads. We didn't engage with problems of race because it didn't affect us on a personal level. It wasn't our battle to fight. Issues of race didn't apply to us because we were white, and white, after all, isn't a color. White is a bland, neutral tone, the lone hue in a rainbow palate that doesn't fit into a category, for *it* is a category in and of itself. Whether at school, at church, or in the workplace, when it came to conversations of race or discussions of racial diversity, our voices didn't count. It didn't matter what we thought because it wasn't about us: race was for people who had color in their skin and not for white people who looked like us.

Sometimes it did affect us, though. It affected Mom when the seasonal calendar for migrant workers made her students miss weeks and months at a time, when they fell so far behind she saw they didn't stand a chance in the traditional system. It affected Dad when the job he felt he rightly deserved went to a person of color instead of to him, when the effects of affirmative action in the late 1980s fell directly onto the two things he couldn't change about himself: that he'd been born white and that he'd been born male. And on Thursday nights, it affected us kids when we weren't allowed to watch *The Cosby Show*.

"Why can't we watch it, Dad?"

"Look at how white people are portrayed, Cara! Look at how they're made to be the bad guys!"

Dad begged us to see the show through his eyes, to see how the comedy made him feel like the nastiest villain of all, purposefully made to look dumb and ignorant against the cast's main characters. To my father, it wasn't a matter of black and white, of pitting one race or one people group against another, but it was a matter of political agendas masked by pop culture's facade. When a job promotion went to someone with fewer qualifications than him who also happened to have darker skin than him, Dad passed along the only truth he knew, a truth of reverse discrimination, where racism did not exist but preferential treatment did. And *The Cosby Show* did not seem to help our plight.

But when Dad had a Thursday night meeting at church, we kids got full control of the lone television in our house. Turning the dial to channel 8, the local NBC affiliate, we closed our eyes when the opening credits came on and threw back our heads, just like we imagined everyone else in America was doing too. We played our faux saxophones, dancing around the living room and competing to see who could yell out Vanessa's and Rudy's real names before the credits flashed on the bottom of the screen. We imagined what it would be like to live in an upscale brownstone in the middle of New York City instead of in a one-story craftsman outside the suburbs of Salem, Oregon. We moaned when Mrs. Huxtable caught Dr. Huxtable sneaking another midnight hoagie, and we wondered whether Mom and Dad would also take all the furniture out of our bedrooms if we tried to make it in the real world as models. Would our dad start chewing on a cigar, just like Harley Weewax, landlord of Real World Apartments did when he was talking to his new tenant, Theo? Would our dad rent us a furniture-less room for twenty-four whole hours too?

But we kept these questions to ourselves. Additional conversations about a television family that was somehow just like us yet worlds apart from us stayed in our minds, never finding their way to the dinner table.

The stories of my childhood played like a film reel in my mind as I sat on James' couch that first night, each glimpse into the past like the flash powder of a vintage camera. As I listened to his stories and saw pictures of his father's legacy, it hit me. I realized that I *did* have a perspective on race, even if it was a perspective I hadn't much thought about or wanted to engage in, even if I hadn't really thought it applied to me. This hadn't ever been the case for James, though, nor had it likely been the case for the students and friends of color I worked with on a daily basis. They grew up with a perspective about race.[1]

I grew up with a perspective that exempted me from the conversation. The weather we talked about. Mom's homemade clam chowder soup with extra bits of bacon we talked about. The funniest joke we'd ever heard, the one Dad told about peanut butter getting stuck to the roof of your mouth, we talked about. But talking about the color of someone else's skin wasn't exactly the *crème de la crème* of dinner table conversation, let alone a message our teachers or youth group leaders eagerly engaged us with. Instead, we volleyed between shouts of a colorblind rhetoric and squeaky choruses of "Jesus Loves the Little Children."

"Children," Mr. Perry, my elementary school principal, said into the microphone, "if we are one thing, we are . . ." Mr. Perry paused. "Colorblind! We are colorblind. We do not see color. Say it with me now, COLORBLIND!" A deafening roar erupted in the gymnasium, six hundred heads raised toward the ceiling, screaming and shouting earnest truths of racial indifference. Like many of our peers across America, the administration didn't want to get racial equality wrong, so they erred on the side of not seeing color at all, the movement itself a reaction to heightened divisions of race less than two decades before.

Thinking back to that moment, I wonder what it must have felt like for my nonwhite peers, for the handful of students of color crammed into the gym that day too. Was it comforting to hear that their friends, their teachers, and even their principal no longer saw them by the outside color of their skin? Or did it feel more like a loss, like the most obvious part of their identity had been swept under a rug of good intentions? Years later, I pored over articles about how children as young as six months old notice differences in race and make changes accordingly. In one study, infants were shown a series of photographs of different faces, each face a contrasting hue of melanin's beauty. Babies stare longer at a picture of someone of a different race because they're trying to make sense of the differences before them.[2] Were my eyes any different, even if a colorblind reel ran through my mind?

Alongside this memory lived the tension of a song, a tune so deeply embedded within my soul I later wondered if the words were ever actually true to me. I stood on the front steps of the church sanctuary, a white Easter hat with a pink ribbon atop my head, a flowered dress sewn by my mother perfectly fitted to my prepubescent body. Hearts beating, palms sweaty, we steadied ourselves to sing the tune written on our hearts, the song of a God who loves the little children, "red and yellow, black and white." As we sang, we didn't picture ourselves sitting serenely at the feet of Jesus, but we saw ourselves slapping high fives and giving hugs and telling our best jokes to him. Faces of every color under the sun crowded around the holy man, a Crayola pack of skin tones gathered before the one who loved without a list of requirements. Without even knowing it, opposing beliefs of seeing and not seeing took up room next to one another in my mind, vying for attention, making me wonder what I was supposed to say and not say, do and not do, see and not see when it came to race.

Lost in my thoughts that first night in James' living room, I looked away, eyes fixed on a corner of the coffee table as equal thoughts of knowing the truth, yet not really knowing any truth at all flooded my mind. My truth was a single, limited perspective: a perspective filled with good intentions, but a perspective of whiteness, nonetheless, and I hadn't ever taken the time to realize there might be another side to the story. Staring ignorance in the eye, I vowed to enter into the conversation, because whether or not James and I had a fourth date, that night in his living room did something in me. I couldn't turn back now. My eyes had seen something I hadn't ever seen before, and I desperately wanted to keep seeing it, even if it meant learning to see color all over again.

CHAPTER 4

Well, I Love You

James and I continued to hunker down, with each other and with discoveries of how we operated as a couple. A month or two into dating, he stood on my front porch early one Saturday morning, a gigantic box wedged between hip and doorframe.

"Well, good morning! And what do we have here?" I asked him, excited about the hike we had planned, unaware of the gift he held in his hands.

"I saw you had only that one pot, the one with a lid that didn't seem to match, so I bought you a new set," he replied. My eyes filled with tears: Who was this man? It was as if a laser beam connected his heart to mine, his ability to sense my needs before I even knew how to communicate them his superpower.

"Seriously, who are you and what planet did you come from?" I joked, unable to believe my luck for what seemed like the hundredth time in the short while we'd been dating. I wrapped my arms around his waist, and we stood there dazzled by the simple profundity of having found one another. A couple of minutes later, loading my car up with snacks and water bottles and a rather excitable border collie, we unknowingly got ready to conquer the ultimate relationship test. We were about to get lost in the woods together.

A few hours into the hike, the words of a spiritual mentor rang in my ears: "If you want to know whether your relationship will stand the test of time, just go on a road trip or somehow get lost together." Having counseled hundreds of couples before marriage, he gave the directive with an almost jolly sense of knowing. When horns are blaring and GPS directions stink, or when trail markers all seem to loop around the same murky green pond in the southwest corner of a nature preserve, one's true identity emerges. The two of us were no exception, as evidenced by the following scientific analysis of two subjects.

> **Subject A:** Staring at the map gripped between his sweaty hands, a raw determination emerges in the hope of pinpointing his location. The subject looks at the map, then he points with index finger toward the horizon, which he believes holds their best chance of survival. The pair has, after all, been hiking for hours by this time. Although they should be nearing the end of this period of physical exertion, neither subject can locate the single path necessary to return them to their point of origin. When pinpointing the location fails, the subject grabs the water bottle from his backpack and takes one final swig. He begins talk of rationing the goods and preparing for the worst before tucking the map into the back pocket of his REI khaki shorts. Finally, placing hand to forehead, he scans the hills for shelter and begins to pray aloud.

> **Subject B:** Bending to scratch the canine's neck, she pours the remaining drops from her water bottle into the dog's mouth. Ever an optimist, she believes the trail marker to be around the next corner and notes a surge of energy in her body when she embraces this attitude. When the previously studied subject

seems to act concerned about the murky green pond they continue to circle, she yawns and stretches her arms: *Oh, to be alive! Oh, to be outside in nature, under the umbrella of creation!* Believing that the spirit of the hiking gods will show them the way, she gazes toward the hills for another human being she can befriend and ask for directions.

As luck (or as scientific analysis) would have it, we didn't have to put up shelter in the woods that night, nor did we have to ration any of our water or food. Instead, a kindly trio of hikers crested the hill a couple of minutes later and pointed out a most obvious trail marker we had somehow missed. With one finger on the map and another pointing toward the sky, James followed the path all the way back to the car, Mr. Darcy and I skipping in syncopation behind him.

By Thanksgiving, I knew James wasn't dating anyone else and someday intended to pull a Beyoncé on my ring finger. I had spent the previous week outside Tijuana, Mexico, speaking to a group of eighty-five high school students determined to spend their holiday digging ditches and mixing concrete. By the end of our time together, although my entire body ached from physical labor, all I wanted was to hear James' voice on the other end of the phone. As we inched toward the US line, I didn't think about the ease with which I could pass from one border city to another, let alone about casting a biblical vision of immigration rights for the marginalized and the oppressed. Instead, I thought about James and James alone. Staring at my cell phone, I willed his text messages and voicemails to appear. When a string of notifications finally popped up, I couldn't have cared less about my aching bones or about taking a shower for the first time in a week. There, from the other end of a pixelated screen, his presence encompassed me, simultaneously surrounding and expanding in my heart. Maybe that's when I knew I was in, that the relationship algorithm of an online dating service had actually worked for us. By the time James and I reunited twenty-four hours later, I didn't want anything or anyone but him. And when, at the end of the night, I mustered the courage to ask whether he was still seeing anyone else on the side, his reply was simple.

"My dear, I'm not dating anyone else, and I don't intend on dating anyone else either." I looked at him and grinned. We had graduated to calling each other dear by that point, but his declaration was news to me.

"You're planning on marrying me, aren't you?" I replied. His smile was the only answer I needed. I was going to marry the man someday.

Around the same time, I figured it best to beg my parents to travel from Oregon to California to meet James. I'd already called them with news that extended beyond the likes of their border collie granddog or the everyday musings of my job in ministry. This time, our conversation involved a real live man their daughter was dating.

"Well," I said the first time I told them about James, taking a deep breath. "I've met someone and he's great and he's black and his name is James Meredith, oh, and did I tell you that his dad is also a man named James Meredith—maybe you remember him from the 1960s?" The words tumbled out of my mouth in a single breath, an abrupt waterfall of information from the daughter who hadn't so much as mentioned a word of her dating life in nearly a dozen years, give or take. It's not that I hadn't wanted my parents to know about this part of my life, but when at nineteen I'd brought home a boy I thought was The One, who quickly turned out not to be The One, I put up walls in my heart. I wouldn't risk love, at least not until I held a guarantee of love in return. I quickly became the three-date wonder, stringing along and being strung along by a chain of boys, always sure to keep my heart at a safe distance.

"Uh, did you hear me?" I asked my parents, my words breaking the silence between us.

"Well, yes," my mom quickly replied. "That's wonderful. And yes, why, I remember James Meredith!"

"James Meredith! Well, that name sure does take me back," Dad added. "And yes, good, good." Our conversation was brief, even though I wanted to ask them whether they were at all surprised by my news or taken off guard when it came to expectations of my future partner. Did it matter that James was a black man and Cara was a white woman? Were they really, actually okay with my dating someone who wasn't white? I wanted to know if James broke a mold or an image set in their minds, a picture pinned to their earliest memories and predictions for me. But I didn't. I let the conversation take its course, moving on to the quilt Mom was sewing for a hospice organization and the ribs Dad had mastered on the backyard smoker.

Years later, I called them on a Tuesday afternoon and asked if they remembered their reaction to my news. "Well, we weren't surprised by who you were dating," my mom replied. "We knew that's where your direction was heading," my dad added, his words a nod to another black man I'd dated before I met James. "But that time was different because you called us. You wanted us to know. And we knew we had to take your words seriously." Although I wasn't privy to their conversations in the months after that phone call, I would wonder if they wrestled with a new sort of reality, with a man their daughter couldn't seem to get enough of. I would wonder if thoughts of James and me occupied a space in their minds they hadn't ever had to think about before. But whether or not they were ready, they would inevitably meet their future son-in-law just a couple of months later.

*A*s the holidays approached, I felt a twinge of pride: I had successfully convinced my parents to visit me, their only unmarried child, for the holiday season. I'd grown used to the rhetoric, to the priorities parents tend to place on their grandchildren and on newly acquired sons- and daughters-in-law. But I also knew that it didn't matter whether a significant other was in the picture. I deserved to have my parents spend Christmas with me, and now they would get to meet James face to face.

It was just another Thursday night at The Macaroni Grill. My parents and I got there a few minutes early for our reservation. James, stuck in bumper-to-bumper traffic on the 101, had called to say he would be a few minutes late.

"He should be here any minute now," I said to them, nervous for both of our sakes. More than anything, I wanted them to like him, to approve of him, to think the world of him.

"Oh, I already met him!" my father exclaimed, wiping his hands in the air, almost in an act of superiority.

"I'm sorry, what?" I replied, nearly spitting out the water I'd just sipped.

"I met him in the men's room! I looked over, and right there at the next urinal was a nice looking black man. 'You must be James!' I said to him. 'You must be Dan,' he replied. He's a very nice young man, I'd say."

"Dad, you didn't."

"I did!"

"But men don't talk to each other, let alone look at each other, in the men's room—that's like the number one rule!"

"I don't know what rule you're talking about, Cara. Besides, how many times have *you* frequented the men's room? Oh, hi, James!" And with that, my father stood up and gripped hands with James, perhaps for the second time that evening. Mortified, I shook my head. This was not how I envisioned the "meet the parents" moment, but after I introduced James to my mother moments later, one thing was clear: my man had charmed the socks off them. Just like me, they were smitten by his presence, unable to get enough of the one who had captured my heart.

A few days after Christmas, James and I were at San Francisco's Orpheum Theater, gripping sweaty hands across a shared arm console. Within minutes, the lights would darken and the curtains would rise on *Wicked,* but first, we would have a conversation that would change our lives.

"Are you excited?" I asked, hopeful he would enjoy the theater as much as me. I had grown up on the stage, on particleboard platforms in elementary school gymnasiums and on the front steps of the church sanctuary. As a high school student, I belted out show tunes as the town floozy in *Brigadoon* and fancied myself a hip-swishing bee-bop girl in *Little Shop of Horrors.* And as an adult, I saved for tickets to various shows traveling through the Bay Area. This was a part of me I wanted James to understand and maybe come to enjoy as well.

"Yes, of course, although football will still rate higher in my book," he said, winking and squeezing my hand. *Yeah, yeah, yeah,* I thought. Try as I might, there were things we would never hold in common, a love of the pigskin being one of them. But I also couldn't get enough of the man.

"You're so cute, I could just squeeze your cheeks and tell you that I love you!" I blurted, hand quickly cupping my mouth, eyes widening. I had said it. I had said "I love you," even though I hadn't planned to say it right then, even though I had been waiting for him to say it first.

"Well, I love you," he replied simply, squeezing my hand in affirmation. Right then the lights went out in the auditorium, as if by magic, as if Eros had smashed the bulbs himself. My eyes filled with tears: he loved me and I loved him. Surely, this would be the greatest show of our lives.

*D*eclarations of love rendered me useless to the outside world: thoughts of James filled my mind, cushioned by visions of contentment, of having loved and been loved in return. But holding another person's heart is delicate business, for standing next to a cascade of sentimentality there is a weight of responsibility. Was I willing to hold the pain of his past, his story, his life? Was I willing to let my heart be broken by the things that break his heart, by the pains of injustice I might never understand?

I thought back to one of the first stories James had ever told me, about returning to Mississippi his freshman year of high school: *It will be different this time. They will be different this time.* But his classmates weren't any different when they called him "boy," and they weren't any different when they spit in his face. After a year in Jackson, James reenrolled at Phillips Academy, the highest-ranked private high school in the United States. But somehow pain followed him, even there.

"People would ask me, 'How'd a black boy from Mississippi end up at Andover?'" James said, recalling the story. "Sometimes I'd laugh, but mostly I didn't know what to say. Why would they ask me that question in the first place? The other students didn't believe I was actually or *could* actually be smart enough to be there with them. When I got a better grade on a test, they thought I cheated. When I scored well on the math portion of my SATs and got into an Ivy League school, they assumed my acceptance letter had to do with affirmative action. They didn't believe I also deserved the right to the best education possible. They didn't believe my mind deserved a place among them."

My head shook in sync with his, the pain of his past quickly worming its way into my heart. The more I got to know James, the more his stories seeped into my soul; the more I fell in love with James, the more I realized how I'd lived in a nest of comfort, snuggled among cushions of convenience. I lived effortlessly, easily, playing it safe, both with my heart and with the hearts of those around me. Don't go too deep, don't feel too much. Keep it on the surface, don't let yourself feel the pain. Don't rock the boat by talking about things like race or even by noticing things like race: *We don't pull the race card in this house.* It was something we weren't supposed to do, not as white people and not as Christians.

My family believed in the American dream, just as we believed in a dream-filled gospel of grace. If I studied hard enough for my US history exam, I could get an A. If I practiced piano long enough, I could master Rachmaninoff's Piano Concerto op. 8 no. 2. Someday, after I graduated from college and got my first job, if I just worked hard enough, I could eventually climb the ladder of success. The onus was entirely on me to put forth my best effort, to go above and beyond, to reach for the stars, a fault that had nothing to do with the color of my skin. After all, if race has nothing to do with determination and drive, why bring it into mixed company? Why pollute the water with a most impolite table topic? On top of that lived a religion of flannelgraph Bible stories and choreographed performances of "Jesus Loves Me," a place where grace and mercy reigned supreme, if only I prayed enough, believed enough, and performed enough too. Then, God would love me. Then, God would honor me. Then, God would bless me. Just as grace rolled off my tongue, a religion of individuality governed my heart, a version of Christianity that left no room for racial identities, let alone for a God who lets "justice roll down like waters, and righteousness like an ever-flowing stream."[1]

We weren't *those* kind of Christians. We weren't *that* kind of church.

But loving James meant coming face to face with pain and injustice. Loving him meant entering into brokenness even when it was the last thing I wanted to do, the last thing I wanted to feel. And loving him also meant facing the facts not only of his life but also of the lives of other people in our country with black and brown skin. As I listened to his story, I realized his was the stuff of fact and miracle. After all, according to society, he was not likely to succeed. He, a young black man, had little chance in a system that favored whites, that questioned why and how he even got there in the first place. He heard it in high school, and he heard it in college, and he heard the echoes of the past every day of his life after that: the why's of oppression coming from the mouths of his accusers, from those who considered themselves better than him in every way. But somehow, whether by sheer determination or a force greater than himself, he who'd felt the weight of systemic injustice, of an educational system that allows white boys to succeed without regard while black boys cower in fear of establishments supposedly designed for the well being of all,[2] had thrived in the end.

Somehow, this man had found his way into my life. But loving him, I soon realized, wasn't all sunshine and roses. Loving him also meant embracing pain. And the pain of institutional racism, of living with his father's fame, and of losing his mother at such a young age wasn't something I knew how to handle.

$\mathcal{S}$omewhere along the way, I had missed the boat on letting myself feel pain, on allowing myself to enter into heartache. "Go home. Rent *Beaches* and *Steel Magnolias*. Hole up and watch the movies by yourself until you let yourself cry," a therapist once told me. "But I do cry!" I replied, reminding her of all the times I had cried out of anger and frustration, when things didn't go my way. "You need to let yourself cry because you feel sad, Cara," she said gently. I nodded. When it came to feeling grief, I didn't want to feel sadness, so I did whatever I could to avoid misery altogether. I walked out of the room. I stifled tears. I clamped my lips together, because as long as words didn't come out of my mouth, tears wouldn't fall from my eyes.

The more time I spent with James, though, the more I realized how I had purposefully avoided and distanced myself from conversations of injustice so I wouldn't have to feel its pain or sadness. Thinking about the atrocities of evil didn't leave a good taste in my mouth. Besides, who would choose to focus on darkness when the light of Christ shone around every corner? Like a psalmist before me, I pitched my tent in the land of hope,[3] gladness exuding from the inside out, ecstasy in God my guiding compass. I engaged when I wanted to engage, when conversation seemed to benefit me and the people around me. But when it was to my advantage—because it was always about my advantage—I walked away. Conversations about justice hung disheveled on a coat rack in the back closet, which I visited once, twice, three times a year when I couldn't avoid its presence any longer.

I remembered the days I spent volunteering with an organization that helped women out of the sex industry in Bangkok, Thailand. One afternoon, the director sent my friend Jeannie and me out into the streets: "Can you discreetly take some pictures of customers purchasing women for sex? A dozen or so should work!" We didn't know any better, but we wanted to save the world, we wanted to do good. So we took turns posing near various men, trying to capture the pleasure of satisfaction when fistfuls of Thai baht were exchanged for a woman's outstretched hand, when a customer slung his arm around a young woman's slender waist. Loud, thumping pulses of bass greeted us as we traipsed up and down dirty sidewalks, thoroughly unprepared for the infestation of heartache. Girls and women of all ages beckoned us through darkened doors, offering us hellos and greetings of "how are you today, pretty lady?" But I avoided their stares as we walked, arms and legs sticky with humidity, conscious of their dolled-up faces against the contrast of mascara trailing down my own face, maybe from sweat, maybe from heartache. I ignored their invitations as I snapped picture after picture: What if they took my engagement as a proposition for more? What if they thought *I* wanted to buy their services? Instead, behind the camera's lens, I fixed my gaze on the men who did say yes, on the tourists who followed the workers into their caverns, on the loud and obnoxious Americans sporting thick, gold wedding rings. I wanted my eyes to pierce through their perceived bubble of intimacy, to make the buyers think of the ones they left behind, to guilt them for using these women for sex. Handing the camera to Jeannie, I bent my head toward her and tried to lighten the mood, my penchant for laughter the only thing I could do to avoid the darkness that seemed to accompany every step.

Less than a year before, Jeannie and I had stood in a crowd, packed like sardines into The Fillmore, an iconic San Francisco concert venue. We usually saw bluegrass shows: after all, the twangy sounds of the Appalachian Mountains were built into Jeannie's bones, and she had passed along to me her love of that sound. But that night our bodies swayed to a different kind of music, our hearts alive to the lyrics of David Crowder, his poetic words a balm to our souls. We closed our eyes. We raised our hands and stomped our feet, as if the power of God really was alive in that place.

Then the musician spoke words my mind could never seem to shake, words that haunted me in Bangkok and on the San Francisco Peninsula and now in conversations with James.

"Compassion is when we're all sitting on the side of a river watching people drown and responding by pulling people out. But justice is when someone pokes their head up and says, 'You know what? I'm going to go upstream to see who keeps throwing everyone into the river.'"[4] Justice I understood halfway around the world when the pain of Soi Cowboy oozed like a sore, when oppression blared in flashing neon lights, in the hazy smoke of cigarettes and marijuana pipes, in the pulse of *sex, sex, sex* everywhere. There, I could easily see the place on the muddy shore upstream where women were thrown into the water. I could pinpoint where flailing arms and drowning bodies began, where a girl first believed her worth was determined by the pleasure she could give.

But injustice in my own back yard? That I couldn't understand. Issues of justice didn't seem to apply to me, nor did they seem to apply to my job as a nonprofit outreach director. Although I worked almost exclusively with students of color, my job kept me in the spiritual realm. My job was about the heart.

"I kind of get paid to be a professional friend," I'd say whenever someone asked me what I did for a living. I explained how my role allowed me to walk alongside students as a tutor in middle schools and high schools, garnering me opportunities to build friendships with teenagers, friendships that sometimes evolved into conversations about the God who couldn't get enough of them, about the one who loved them more than life itself. Even though I volunteered during after-school hours, helped plan and run evening programs, and rallied other adults in fundraising efforts, I viewed my position, and those students and adult volunteers entrusted to my care, solely through a spiritual lens. We were about introducing teenagers to Christ through relationships. We were about coming alongside students in their worlds and meeting them wherever they were in life. We were about cheering them on for the great and glorious humans they already were, just as we were about raising the funds to help them go to camp in the summer and sometimes in the winter too. There, they could get away from the busyness and the distractions and the hurt that come with being a teenager. They could just be kids again and build a significant relationship with an adult mentor and maybe even with Jesus for the first time in their lives. But as the director, I wasn't about dwelling in the hardships of injustice, at least not in the students' day-to-day lives.

So I didn't ask, when Latinos made up only twenty percent of the student body, why ninety percent of the school's failing students in the after-school tutoring program were Latino. I didn't ask, when African Americans made up only seven percent of the student body, why ninety-eight percent of out-of-school suspensions involved these same students. I didn't ask not because I didn't believe it my place to ask but because I didn't see the problem in the first place. I didn't see how injustice had already taken root in the community I loved, with the students I had come to care for so deeply.

Students failed because they didn't try hard enough, I thought.

Students got suspended because they didn't follow the rules, I mused.

Besides, my job wasn't about heading upstream to see who was throwing these kids into the water. My job was about showing them compassion when they flopped onto the shore, breathless, beaten, nearly drowned.

But when James ripped his heart open and told me stories about a system that couldn't have cared less if he failed, got suspended, or ended up in prison, I saw that my response needed to involve more than a mere offering of compassion. I needed to learn how to respond with a heart bent toward justice, how to search for the spot in the weeds where the problem first began.

*H*ere, read this," James wrote me in an email as he passed along a weekly installment of stories and articles related to systemic injustice. Real examples from my own back yard, including stories and statistics I had never paid attention to before, began to take root within me. Alone in my backyard cottage, with Mr. Darcy snuggling at my feet, I began to read. Sometimes I couldn't take in more than a paragraph or two: the subject was too hard to gulp down, too painful for me to absorb. And sometimes, I just didn't get it. I loved James, I reminded myself when my eyes started to glaze over and I was overwhelmed by all the new information. "I love you, I love you, I love you," I'd say when we talked on the phone or met up for a weeknight meal. Words could not express, no matter how many times I said it or how eloquently I tried, how much his love had changed me. I wanted *our* love to be enough, just as I wanted the power of our ebony and ivory identities to be enough to rid the world of racism and injustice and oppression.

But our love wasn't enough to move firmly rooted systems, especially not when it came to issues like education, housing, economics, and the criminal justice system. Love wasn't enough when I pictured James walking up to schoolhouse doors as a child, his peers staring at him, arms folded over their chests, eyes slit defiantly. *You don't belong here, boy!* And love wasn't enough when I thought about the white, middle-class neighborhood I grew up in, a place so different from his own. Tree-lined sidewalks encouraged squeals and childlike play, beckoning me to overturn every stone and explore every corner from the wheels of my bicycle. There wasn't a place I couldn't explore, a face I couldn't trust. And love also wasn't enough when I saw how, more often than not, the young black and brown boys I worked with were watched and followed and accused of crimes they hadn't committed. I knew it was time for me to understand.

I thought about the walks I took with Mr. Darcy, how dilapidated Section 8 apartments were stacked next to five-million-dollar mansions, the neighborhoods I lived in a place where wealth and poverty seemed to greet one another with a holy kiss.[5] But I also thought about the color divide I hadn't taken the time to notice before, about the many rules that had been bent for the sake of prejudice. In a way, James' family seemed to escape some of the housing discrimination laws established in the United States in the thirties and forties, laws that only helped to further segregation in an already divided country.[6]

In 1923, James' grandfather Moses "Cap" Meredith quit his job as a sharecropper and purchased eighty-four acres of land to farm on his own.[7] Although he never made more than three hundred dollars a year, he called himself a rich man, bucking discrimination by refusing to answer to anyone but himself. But Cap's story felt like the exception rather than the rule. I remembered attending a forum at a church in San Francisco on the effects of gentrification. One woman stood up to tell the story of her parents, who dreamed of owning a home in Chicago in the late fifties but couldn't buy one because of zoning laws and because they didn't qualify for a loan. In 1963, when some friends offered to purchase a house for them, her parents called it a partial hand of luck, even though their names wouldn't be on the deed for years to come. Why the partial hand of luck? The woman's parents were black. The couple who purchased a house for them, because the law allowed it, was white. Even though Congress passed fair housing laws five years later, the damage had already been done. "We cannot let unfair housing practices like gentrification happen in our city too," she'd shouted into the microphone. Now I felt like I understood part of the story just a little bit more.

But I also thought about how our love wouldn't be enough when it came to the wealth gap between blacks and whites. I didn't think the conversation applied to me, mostly because I was a single woman trying to make ends meet on a ministry salary in one of the most expensive areas of the country. At the start of every month, I sat at my kitchen table, a stack of bills to my right, a calculator to my left. I pinched pennies. I shopped at secondhand stores. When I didn't know whether Mr. Darcy and I would make it to the end of the month, I ate cereal for every meal. "I don't know how we're going to do it, MD," I'd say when no one else was around, when the shame of debt spiraled around me. But *this* conversation wasn't about me, nor was it about the choice I had made to live at a particular income level: just as blacks are twice as likely as whites to be employed in low-wage jobs, African Americans are also twice as likely to be unemployed.[8] Whether or not I wanted to believe it, overall wealth would continue to swing in my favor: even if I came upon hard times, over the years, I would still end up with more net assets and less debt simply because of the color of my skin. This had nothing to do with the financial choices I had made or would someday make, but existed entirely by birthright alone.

I also thought about how our love wouldn't be enough when it came to education and to the criminal justice system, two threads bound in a single knot. A phrase of my childhood echoed through my mind: "If at first you don't succeed, try, try again!" Like my choice to live at a particular income level, the onus for my success lay entirely on me. I just had to try harder, do better, and network with the right people. But these words of individualization, words that whispered guarantees of success as long as I did my part, weren't as universal as I'd hoped.

"I think about the kids of color I work with on a daily basis," my friend C. J. said to me, hands cupped around the mug of steaming tea in front of her. She and I worked for the same organization, although on opposite ends of the San Francisco Bay. "In this broken system, these kids are getting shoved through. I can't tell you how many times each one of them has been pulled aside for a conversation with their school counselor. And do you know what the adult says to them? 'You're not going to college. You're not going to college. You're not going to college.'" Her voice trembled as memories resurfaced, her fingers jabbing the air around her with each accusation as tears welled in her eyes.

"Every time they're pulled into an office or a classroom, this is what they hear," she said. "Meanwhile, the white kids are told to dream big, because they're going to Harvard, to Stanford, to Cal. That's institutionalized racism for you, in Berkeley, California, the most progressive city in America." As she spoke, I thought about the tutoring program's end-of-year barbeque a couple of weeks before. I was in charge of games for the evening, and after I explained the rules of Capture the Flag, a couple of boys asked me not once but twice if it was *really* okay for them to play the game. "Why wouldn't you be allowed to play Capture the Flag?" I responded, not understanding why a sixteen-year-old African American boy couldn't run around an unknown neighborhood after dark, hiding behind bushes and next to cars, in search of a neon flag. This was a school-sponsored event. Hadn't my permission been enough?

But I also remembered the stories a group of middle school

students had told me about place, about the hallways and underhangs and corners to avoid if you didn't want to be called certain names. I hadn't said anything in response, at least not then, but my eyes said it all: I clearly did not understand the meaning of their words. "You know, mean things, racist things, things you're not supposed to say because they're wrong," the girls explained, flicking their pencils in the air as if to shoo away marks of racism. "Wait," I replied. "You mean, other kids say racist words to you because of the color of your skin, because you're Latina?" They nodded their heads numbly, my unknowing perhaps just as paralyzing as their knowing. Years later, when I read that black students are three times as likely as white students to be suspended or expelled, it didn't come as much of a surprise.[9] Maybe this time I wasn't so numb, the effect of blatant racism not nearly as shocking as when I heard of it the first time.

Regardless, it wasn't so hard to imagine the connection between education and the criminal justice system, how being on your best behavior and avoiding potentially negative places and situations might mean escaping the possibility of a jail cell altogether.[10] I'd never had to think about escaping the system, because there was never anything for me to run away from in the first place. But now, staggering statistics had staked a personal claim on my heart, and I begged for relief, for some piece of hope.

"This isn't you," I remember saying to James. "You've done well. You've been successful. You've risen above!" I wanted to make the man I loved an exception to the rules of injustice, but I couldn't let his circumstances blind me from the truth. If only I could do something. If only I could fight back and fix the problem, because seeing the big picture, finding a solution, and fixing the problem was what I did. It's what I did in ministry, and it's what I did as a white person. White people fix things, end of story. But all of this felt out of my reach and beyond my control. I couldn't fix deeply rooted systems of injustice by slapping on a bandaid or offering a cheery Christian platitude about Jesus taking the wheel.

I'd been so scared to let myself feel the pain of the world around me, but if I loved James, pain would inevitably become part of my story too. If I loved James, then I had to take a risk on things that hurt, on things that might cause me to feel uncomfortable. And if I loved James, then his story and his people, his oppression and his people's oppression would someday become inextricably linked with mine.

I could accept that. But that didn't stop me from wanting to run from all the pain.

CHAPTER 5

Three Years in Mississippi

*L*ess than a week after saying "I love you" to each other for the first time, James and I found ourselves declaring our resolutions for the coming year over slices of greasy pizza in the North Beach district of San Francisco.

"So what's your New Year's resolution?" I asked him, melted cheese dribbling down my chin as I ravenously chomped an enormous bite of sourdough crust.

"I don't really believe in resolutions."

"You don't believe in resolutions? But this is America. And Americans *do* believe in resolutions at the start of a new year."

"Well, then, maybe I'm not American," he replied and winked at me. "Anyway, I don't believe in making resolutions, but I do believe in setting goals for myself." I rolled my eyes as a smirk spread across my face. Everything about him—from speech to thought to action—was so overtly practical sometimes. But I loved that about him.

"Okay, then, let's talk about *goals* for the new year. I'll go first: I want to go running with Mr. Darcy more," I said, wiping tomato sauce from my chin. I dreamed of giving my dog the exercise his canine body needed. We would run every day that year, or at least three or four days a week. I thought of what would happen to my body as it logged a stack of miles, week after week, year after year. Toned legs. A slimmer, trimmer me. A legitimate six-pack in my midregion and a complete transformation of my body, set to begin the very next day. "So what about you, James?"

"I plan on marrying you this year," he replied. I gasped, dropping my pizza onto the cardboard plate, my dream of running four miles a day suddenly forgotten.

*A*ccording to twenty-first-century dating standards, our dating relationship was the epitome of fast and furious, but we couldn't have cared less. We had found each other and that was all that mattered. Besides eventually putting a ring on my fourth finger and throwing together a wedding celebration, there was one more thing we needed to do: we needed to fly to Jackson, Mississippi, to meet James' side of the family. As sure as I was about James, though, I wasn't so sure about the Meredith family. How would his father's prominence affect us, if at all? Although our differences intrigued me, was I too different from James? And would his family, a cornerstone of the black community, accept me, a white woman? A deeper, nagging question of pain scraped away at the insides of my heart: loving James meant embracing the pain of his story and his life, as well as letting my heart and mind enter into the reality of the injustices I hadn't chosen to see. But when it came to the Meredith family, could I ever fully embrace the sores of racial inequality that blatantly marked their story?

Some of my questions found answers the moment I walked through the door of my future in-laws' home. James' father rose from his chair to shake my hand, a hint of a smile pulling at the corner of his mouth, a sparkle dancing in his eyes. James' stepmother, Judy, threw formality aside and pulled me toward her, while James' half sister Jessica waved from the kitchen, fully occupied by a homemade meal, her gift to us that first night. With delighted squeals, Jessica's four young children—Janae, Jaylah, Jameria, and little baby James—ran toward us, wrapping their arms around our legs and waists. Within minutes, we started playing Hide and Go Seek with the children, discovering every nook and cranny of the patriarch's old house.

"Aunt Cara, you count and we'll hide!" the girls directed me, five minutes into our arrival. With Uncle James trailing behind, they scurried to different rooms as I covered my eyes and started counting.

"Ready or not, here I come!" I yelled.

"Ready!"

"Ready!"

"Ready!"

A chorus of echoes filled the hallways, each child making her presence known to she who was seeking. Stifling a laugh, I wiped tears from my eyes, already smitten by this place and by these people.

A day or two later, James and I, along with his father, crammed a couple of the girls into his father's Toyota Corolla and drove the hour and twenty minutes north to Kosciusko. The girls and I played Follow the Leader, tiptoeing over fallen logs and peering into the window of the decrepit log cabin where Granddaddy spent the first seventeen years of his life. The family still owned the one hundred and twenty acres of land, its soil rich for growing pine trees, among other kinds of timber. Meanwhile, James and his father walked together, engaged in private conversation.

"You're rather like the boys' mother," James' father finally declared, the only thing he said to me that day, and one of the few times I'd ever hear him mention his former wife. For his father, for the children, and for the rest of the family, even though I hadn't yet married into the family, there was no doubt in their minds: Aunt Cara was in, simply because she was loved by Uncle James.

A day or two later, James and I sat in his uncle's back yard, icy cold drinks pressed against our cheeks to ward off the heat.

"You know, it's not so much about you, a white woman, entering this family," Uncle Arthur noted, "but it's about you realizing the impact one man's father had on the world." His fingers pointed first toward me and then toward the man I loved before continuing. Arthur's pride in and esteem for his brother's accomplishments were obvious, but was I willing to understand the impact? Was I willing to do the hard work and dig into the story that might someday be my own?

I nodded, startled by Arthur's intuition. James and I hadn't asked him about the obvious, about our interracial relationship or about my being the first white woman to marry into the immediate family. But he spoke an answer I didn't know I'd wanted to hear: my white skin didn't matter, but the ignorance that sometimes accompanies whiteness did. In that moment, I bit the gravity of his words, tasting the significance of one man's influence while simultaneously wondering if I could handle the pain that inevitably comes with knowing.

I began reading everything I could get my hands on. Starting with Google, I made my way from Wikipedia to forgotten, musty encyclopedias on back shelves of the San Francisco Public Library. A stack of books, courtesy of Amazon and my sweetheart, soon filled my bedside table, my newfound appetite to know the man behind *my* man insatiable. James Howard Meredith was born in 1933, in Kosciusko, Mississippi, to Moses "Cap" and Rosie Meredith. The third of ten children, he was named J. H., a first and middle name purposefully given to help assuage subservient interactions with white people. At that time in the Deep South, black people were expected to address white people by adding a title such as mister, missus, or miss to their names.[1] As author and historian Ann Bausum writes, this reinforced a hierarchical racial social order: not only did white people *not* have to address blacks in the same way, but white people often created childish nicknames for black people—nicknames, she states, that could last a lifetime. "Meredith's parents chose not to give him a proper name, such as James, which could have become a source of humiliation if whites called him Jimmy instead."[2]

Additionally, and perhaps more important, J. H. believed he'd been born to pass on the legacy of his great-grandfather, the last leader of the Choctaw Nation. This was an honor given to the third-born son, and J. H. breathed in its grave significance, passing it on to *his* thirdborn son, the man who eventually became my husband. J. H., along with his parents and siblings, believed education was the best way to fight white supremacy, so they did what they had to do: they began by walking four miles to school every day.

As a child, I sometimes dreaded the two-and-a-half-block walk to my elementary school. "When I was a kid," my mother would say, "I had to walk two miles to and from school, uphill each way. In the snow, the rain, the sleet." "Mom, you didn't *get* snow in Fresno," I'd reply, nodding my head in solemn mockery, cognizant of the lush and fertile farmland of California's central valley. "Well, quit your whining and bundle up," she'd reply as I positioned myself in winter coat, mittens, scarf, and knit beanie.

But walking forty miles a week was no joke to J. H., nor was moving to Florida his senior year of high school to obtain the best education possible. It wasn't until graduation that he chose the name

James Howard for himself, a requirement for enlistment in the United States Air Force. Although he spent time at various air force bases in the US and met his first wife, Mary June, on a base in Missouri, his time in Japan shaped him the most. There, for the first time in his life, he didn't experience racism. There, racial hierarchy didn't control every nook and cranny of society. From government to education, businesses to religion, being a black man wasn't an issue. There, he was free, and it was through this experience that he began to act on his long-held dreams: he could fight the strongholds of white supremacy by tackling them from the very top of the system. He could free himself of the adjectives affixed to his identity, for he would be not a black man but simply a man. He could fight for his right to an equal education by becoming the first black man to graduate from the highest collegiate institution in his home state. Somehow, he who had been oppressed would stand up to the oppressor by fighting the entire state of Mississippi. But perhaps more significant, he wouldn't do it on his own.

After serving nine years in the air force, in the fall of 1960 James, Mary June, and their two-year-old son, John, moved home to Jackson, capital of the Magnolia State. There, joy and hope intermingled with sadness: "Joy because I have once again lived to enter the land of my fathers, the land of my birth, the only land in which I feel at home,"[3] but sadness because of the subhuman role the black man was forced to play. The young marrieds enrolled as full-time students at Jackson State University, a historically black college. With credits he obtained from three other institutions during his time in the air force, James enrolled as an advanced junior. Whenever anyone asked him what he wanted to do with his life, he replied, "I want to be a man, run for governor of the state of Mississippi, and get a degree from the University of Mississippi, in reverse order."[4] He wanted to rid the adjective *colored* from all descriptions of himself, empower blacks with the right to vote in his home state, and break racism's grip on institutional education.

A three-year journey began: in a strategy designed to hold the Kennedy administration accountable to the civil rights platform President Kennedy ran on during his election, James Meredith reached out to Ole Miss the day after Kennedy's inauguration. The University of Mississippi registrar, Robert Ellis, enthusiastically acknowledged his ample qualifications as a transfer student upon receipt of his first letter: "We are very pleased to know of your interest in becoming a member of our student body,"[5] Ellis stated. With that response, the real work began.

Meredith requested transcripts be sent to the university from all previous educational institutions. He met with local activist Medgar Evers. He penned a letter to Thurgood Marshall, director of the NAACP Legal Defense Fund. And ten days after sending the first inquiry, he wrote another letter to the registrar, stating in part, "I am an American—Mississippi—Negro citizen. With all of the presently occurring events regarding changes in our old educational system taking place in our country in this new age, I feel certain that this application does not come as a surprise to you. I certainly hope that this matter will be handled in a manner that will be complimentary to the University and the state of Mississippi."[6]

His application for admission was missing one piece: the names of six university alumni. This, of course, was a no-brainer. Given racial relations in the South at the time, if every graduate from the university was white, James Meredith did not actually know any alumni. So he provided letters of character reference from six individuals—all of whom happened to be black—as a substitute.

Four days later, he received a telegram from Ellis: his application for admission had been denied. He should not appear for registration.

The fight had begun.

*H*is story stops me in my tracks. I pause and ask myself whether I would have done the same had I been in his shoes. The benefits of being a white, straight, Christian woman have always been mine. Even if I feel I haven't always received equal treatment in the workplace or other contexts because of my gender, the advantages have always been mine. The right to a quality education, even if it costs me a decade or two of loan repayments? Mine. I can almost be guaranteed a job, my networks of association pleased to see me succeed in the marketplace. The right to marry whomever I choose? Mine. As much as I imagine myself donning a heroine's cape if push comes to shove, and as much as I believe myself capable of leading a charge against the deepest sources of racism, injustice, and misogyny, the fight has always been in my favor.

Oftentimes, I think privilege is all about me—all about the haves and have-nots of my life. But it's actually not all about me. In our American context, it's about those who are not white, who are not straight, who are not Christian, who do not have what I already, naturally possess. "Our privileges are the things not within our own control that push us forward and move us ahead from that starting line," writes activist Luvvie Ajayi.[7] But privilege, as has often been stated, means being born on third base and going through life thinking you hit a triple.

So would I have fought the good fight half a century ago? Would I have refused to take no for an answer, determined to accomplish what I believed I was put on this earth to do? Or would I have taken the registrar's words as a sign and, believing that God opens and closes doors as God sees fit, moved on to the next open door, the next opportunity? I'm sure I would have done the latter. I may have been sad, but I would have chalked up the registrar's rejection as proof that something else was just around the next corner. After all, when the system shouts and screams and yields in your favor, you don't have to be that brave before you get another chance to show off your skills. But the man who eventually became my father-in-law had no choice but to fight, no choice but to continue donning his boxing gloves and stepping into the ring.

*F*ollowing the telegram from Ellis, as well as subsequent communication with the university, including a second refusal of admission, James Meredith received assistance from the NAACP, which assigned prominent civil rights attorney Constance Baker Motley to the case. For nearly eighteen months, the case bounced through various courts. At both the local and state levels, southern judges ruled racism was *not* a part of the University of Mississippi's decision to deny admission. But when the case reached the United States Court of Appeals for the Fifth Circuit, the judge ruled in favor of James Meredith's right to attend the University of Mississippi. Although the state of Mississippi appealed to the Supreme Court, the court upheld the ruling.

James Meredith had officially won the right to attend one of the most staunchly segregated universities in the Deep South.

By this point, he and his wife, June, were still living in Jackson, still attending Jackson State University, and still raising their young son, John. With fall semester quickly approaching, it became evident that he would not be attending the university without federal intervention. Here, various villains enter the story: Mississippi state governor Ross Barnett, who ran on a platform of segregation, escalated threats of exclusion, and "on September 13, 1962, the District Court entered an injunction directing the members of the Board of Trustees and the officials of the University to register Meredith."[8] To Barnett, my father-in-law was merely a pawn to be played in the greater fight of an individual state against the United States government. Also, former general Edwin Walker, who five years earlier, before his resignation from the army, had commanded the troops who insured the integration of the Little Rock Nine under President Eisenhower, issued a war cry of his own: known for his unfaltering conservative values (and no longer under the supervision of the commander in chief), he would not stand for another integration if he had anything to do with it.[9] Additionally, as the integration drew near, various white supremacist groups, like the United Klans of America, began rallying troops from as far away as California and as close as the bordering states—Louisiana, Alabama, and Georgia.

The event became the highlight of national newsreels, and a little more than one hundred years after the first, a new civil war threatened to erupt on American soil. It was the North versus the South, the United States government versus one of its own states, and the University of Mississippi was caught in the middle of it all.

The Kennedy brothers, of course, stood in the center of the controversy. As it escalated, so did their communication with Barnett. They asked. They charmed. They threatened. They tried every tactic in the book, and, finally unable to get a straight answer from the governor, the brothers fined him ten thousand dollars for each day he disobeyed their orders.[10] As head of state, Barnett held ultimate authority, so he, instead of the state, would be held personally accountable. Although he espoused the values of segregation, the cause wasn't worth that much of a financial hit to him and his family. Unbeknownst to the public until the early 1980s, when the FBI released hidden recordings from the Oval Office, the three struck a secret deal: in public, the attention-seeking governor would continue to tout the values of the Old South, ideals that had landed him his position in the first place. He would put up a fight. He wouldn't back down, mostly so he could save face before his constituents. But behind closed doors, Barnett quietly acquiesced to Meredith's presence.

Then, all hell broke loose.

*O*f course, "all hell broke loose" is an American idiom. When the sky rains cats and dogs, felines and canines do not fall from the sky, but it does rain fiercely. When my friend Jerusalem warns me not to slap lipstick on a pig, she refers not to the application of cosmetic products on my future breakfast but instead to not covering up a reality. A pig is a pig is a pig, no matter how much Maybelline you apply to its snout. Likewise, the idiom "a cross to bear" refers to an "unpleasant situation or responsibility that you must accept because you cannot change it."[11] It's rooted in the past, referring to criminals who were made to carry crosses as a form of punishment and to the cross Jesus bore as he carried his death piece up to the Place of the Skull. For James Meredith, becoming the first black man to attend and graduate from an all-white university wasn't merely his cross to bear, it was his divine mission.[12] But fulfilling his destiny meant ushering forth a night of hell. And on the night of September 30, 1962, all hell really did break loose in Oxford, Mississippi.

The world knew what would happen come Monday morning, but they had to survive Sunday night first.

By late afternoon, three hundred US marshals arrived to maintain peace and escort James Meredith to class the next morning, and unbeknownst to the crowd or to anyone else, the marshals had already quietly escorted him into his dorm room. More than three hundred journalists from around the world gathered in the sleepy college town to cover the integration. By late afternoon, Ole Miss students rallied in the Circle at the center of campus, taunting officials. Shortly before 7:30 in the evening, a growing mob of two thousand segregationists from across the country protested his entrance into the university. For many of the protestors gathered that night, it wasn't James Meredith they were protesting. It was the fact that the US government had interfered with the rights of one of its own states, undermining the values of southern culture and the longstanding traditions of a way of life.

But the white people opposed to integration had an even deeper fear. According to William Doyle, author of *An American Insurrection,* that fear was "the sexual hysteria and jealousy of the black man that gripped white Americans since slavery began. It was fear of the dreaded 'miscegenation,' or mixing of the races, that was railed against publicly but often practiced in private by many white males, who for generations had pursued black women."[13] If the US government forced the University of Mississippi to allow blacks to integrate into the all-white school, then the coeds would mix. If the coeds mixed—in classes, in the lunchroom, and at football games—then the coeds might fall in love. And if the coeds fell in love, then the white race would no longer remain untainted.

Fear, of course, has driven the human race since the beginning of time. Christians say the first two humans believed not in the words of their creator but in the lies of a slippery, writhing serpent: "You will not certainly die . . . For God knows that when you eat from it your eyes will be opened, and you will be like God, knowing good and evil."[14] Adam and Eve, eating the fruit of the one tree God had commanded them not to eat from, brought death into the world, and with it fear. They feared they would not be like God, that they would not live forever. They feared the consequences of their naked shame. Fear reigned supreme.

Are we all that different, two thousand years later? Have the Industrial Revolution, postmodernism, and our technological age alleviated fear? Or are we still driven by it?

Whether we are on the internet or sitting around the dining room table, fear swallows our conversations, for we are scared of what we do not know, of what we fail to understand. We're scared of getting hurt, and we're still scared of dying. We're scared of being alone, and we're scared that our love will not be returned. We're scared that something tragic will happen to the ones we love the most, and we're scared that our love will not be enough to save them. We're scared of making mistakes, and we're scared of losing our jobs. We're scared that our retirement pensions (if we have them) will not be enough, and that our paychecks won't stretch to the end of the month. We're scared of terrorists and wildfires, of gun violence and climate change, of abortion rights and Black Lives Matter, and we're scared that our walls aren't high enough to keep the bad guys away.

But sometimes, maybe most of all, we're scared of the other. We fear those who don't look like us, whose experiences are different from our own, whose stories and lives we do not understand. So really, is James Meredith's story all that different from ours, nearly sixty years later?

*O*n the night of the integration, at exactly eight o'clock in the evening, President Kennedy delivered a televised speech to the nation, pleading for peace. At that same moment (unbeknownst to Washington), US marshals fired the first round of tear gas into the mob of protestors. Within an hour, nearly twenty-five hundred rioters attacked the campus, armed with any weapon they could get their hands on. "They carried the weapons of a spontaneous, improvised insurrection—clubs, hunting knives, blackjacks, tire chains. Other rioters with squirrel guns, shotguns, .22s, and high-powered rifles were on their way."[15] They tore loose bricks and chunks of concrete from university buildings, setting fire to and jerry-rigging vehicles they drove into an opposing force of three hundred marshals.

Chaos enveloped the campus, and for what purpose? To preserve the southern way of life or to keep fear of the unknown at bay? Soon tragedy struck: snipers fired from oak, elm, and magnolia trees, killing a French reporter and a bystander, and injuring nearly two-thirds of the marshals. Although the Kennedy brothers had allowed the marshals to fire tear gas, by ten o'clock the marshals still weren't allowed to fire their guns. Perhaps that's when the president realized the severity of the insurrection. According to many historians, the government's action—or lack thereof—regarding the Battle of Oxford (as the riot was later called) came too late, its slowness to recognize the severity of the uprising a mistake that easily could have been avoided.

Soon, nearly fifteen thousand troops from the Mississippi National Guard and the US Army were called in as reinforcements, and an additional sixteen thousand arrived in northern Mississippi thereafter. Working together, they finished driving rioters off the campus by 2:15 in the morning and declared the campus secure four hours later.

Meanwhile, James Meredith slept soundly through the commotion, protected by a team of marshals assigned to his room, the hallway, and the perimeter of the men's dorm. Early in the morning, marshals escorted him to register and to attend his first class, accompanying him every day until he graduated nearly eleven months later.

I paused in my studies, the fruit of learning, listening, and gathering information more than my heart could handle. This pain was real, and this hate was reverberating. The more I read, the more I wondered whether the vitriol and the sorrow ever went away. As a white woman, I'd long believed we lived in a postracial society, in a country so far past racism it had elected a black man to the highest seat in the land. But hate and injustice lie not on the surface but deep within the soil, seeping into the water, affecting every root within reach. The more I got to know the story of James' father, a man "propelled by fierce, stubborn determination, [who] launched a one-man revolt against white supremacy, conducted a bruising, sixteen-month legal struggle, forced the federal courts and the president to his side, squared off against the political, legal and police forces of an entire state, and triggered the greatest constitutional crisis since the Civil War, all to simply honor his rights as an American citizen,"[16] the more I begged for eyes to see everything I had missed.

Holed up at an old wooden table in the back of a public library, I paused in my studies, looking toward the vaulted ceiling. *Lord, give me the eyes to see and the ears to hear the pain and the hurt around me,* I breathed into the musty air. It was a prayer I hadn't often prayed, nor had I ever wished to make it my prayer. I wanted to put a pin in my understanding, just as I wanted someday to be a person who stood up to fear, who didn't back down, who refused to be confined by the lies of injustice in the world around her. But first I had to learn how to listen.

CHAPTER 6

1967, Then and Now

Nearly five months after our first date, James and I spent the day together. It was just another Saturday: we celebrated a friend's engagement party, ran errands, and relaxed with one another in the six-hundred-square-foot cottage I called home. He paced the carpet of the living room, while my toes tapped on the linoleum of the kitchen floor, heads bobbing in unison to the tenor pop of Michael Jackson.

"Uh, Cara, would you come here?" he called, the floor creaking with each of his steps.

"Not right now, love. I'm kind of in the middle of something." My hands dangled over the crockpot, tiny pieces of raw chicken and biscuit dough clinging to my fingers. He cleared his throat.

"Cara MacDonald, would you *please* come here?" Annoyed by his lack of patience and by the fact that he'd called me by my full name (and tacked on a respectful "please" to boot), I glanced over my shoulder and realized that Grandma's Chicken and Dumplings could wait. There, in my living room, a man knelt down on one knee, a tiny black box open before him.

"Are you asking me to marry you?" I blurted. "Hold on!" Rinsing bits of food off my fingers, I rushed at him, hands held high in the air like a surgeon entering the operating room.

He nodded, not saying a word.

"Well, then ask me already!" His expectation of our perfect moment foiled, James popped the question anyway. As he slipped a ring onto my finger, I shouted a triumphant *yes, yes, yes!* over and over again. We were getting hitched.

*A*nother five months flew by, this time preparing for the big day. Young, idealistic and more than slightly naive, we prepared not for a single, extravagant event but for a lifetime of love. Tuesday nights became wedding preparation nights: We created lists of wedding guests; we refined lists of wedding guests. We asked our friend Brian to officiate the wedding, and we begged our spiritual mentors, Russ and Linda, to give us premarital counseling. We wrote down our ceremony musts (Marvin Gaye, him; coconut cupcakes, me), and must-nots (open mic toasts, him; any scriptural references to male headship, me). We sampled every five-dollar bottle of wine Trader Joe's had to offer, addressed and mailed wedding invitations, and scoured the internet for the best porta-potty deal, multiple Honey Buckets a necessary expense for having a wedding on my aunt and uncle's Nevada City front lawn.

When the day finally arrived, there wasn't a thing left to do but utter holy yeses before our communion of saints. The hot August sun beat down upon the red dirt and ponderosa pines of California's Gold Country, driving temperatures into the high nineties as late afternoon approached. Somehow, it felt like we had already known each other our whole lives; we had risked love, with our hearts and with each other. I thought back to a night only a couple of months before. "I don't know if I can do this," I had said to a girlfriend when our relationship felt too heavy for me to hold. I wanted optimism and hope and filtered pictures of happiness, not just for me but for the two of us. I wanted a chorus of Julie Andrews' songs to mark our story, idyllic scenes filled with sunshine and roses and smiles on flowered Scandinavian hillsides. There was no doubt that love marked our story, but pain held a place in our chapters too.

I couldn't help but love James, though. I couldn't imagine a future without his face beside mine, just as I couldn't imagine walking down the aisle toward anyone else. As evening neared, I hid behind an ivied trellis, a microphone in my hand. James and the groomsmen stood at the bottom of the lawn, soon joined by the bridesmaids and two flower women who threw yellow rose petals. The rich alto voices of my cousin Kaitlin and our friend Bianca filled the outdoor grove, their voices the sole accompaniment to the rustling of the pines.

"You done good, kid," my dad said, elbowing me as I sat beside him on a worn wooden bench behind the trellis. I thought about the words shared between us over the years and also about the things not said, about how we tended to keep it safe in our conversations with thoughts of the weather and highlights of our day. For my dad, it wasn't necessarily about his daughter marrying a black man, but it was about his daughter marrying a good man who happened to have brown skin, about the myriad ways James cherished me as a partner and as my father's daughter.

"I'll never forget when James called me on the phone," my dad said, maybe in an attempt to ease my nerves, maybe in an attempt to ease his own. "Asking for someone's hand in marriage is a tradition that's almost extinct now, and I was quite overcome by the fact that he actually did call and ask. And there he was, hemming and hawing, acting all nervous, having trouble getting to the question I knew he wanted to ask. I finally stopped him and said, 'Shoot, man, shoot!'" I smiled at the memory, at hearing the story from his perspective.

"And did he shoot?" I asked.

"He did," Dad replied. Leaning toward him, I linked my arm

into his, watching the freckles of his skin meld into my own. I thought about how he had loved me from the very beginning, and about how, in an almost unexplainable way, we could still be bound by uncanny amounts of sameness and difference. There would still be points of frustration between us, the stories of our varied experiences something that would take a lifetime to unpack, but for now, we had found common ground in the man who stood at the bottom of the aisle, waiting for us to arrive.

As silence entered the grove, my dad and I stood up together. In moments, I would sing myself down the aisle, echoing lyrics I sang in middle school, unaware then of the song's biblical roots. Soon after we first said "I love you," James and I had nestled close to one another on a picnic blanket, the whipping wintery winds of the Northern California coast almost too much for our bodies to bear. "Can I sing you a song?" I'd asked him after a couple of minutes of quiet. Staring at the ocean as I sang, I felt his heartbeat as I leaned against his chest, the breath of his mouth against my neck.

> Set me as a seal upon your heart,
> as a seal upon your arm,
> for love is strong as death.
>
> Many waters cannot quench love,
> neither can the floods drown it,
> neither can the floods drown it.[1]

When I finished and looked up at him, tears trailed down his cheeks. "Never stop singing that to me," he whispered, wrapping his arms around me and pulling me toward him. Nodding, I vowed to make the song our lullaby of love, for I knew and I believed in the power of love, in an engulfing, mighty kind of love that can change the world. But as I stood behind the trellis and steadied myself to sing, fear swept over me.

My heart felt like it was going to explode out of my body, the pounding of my pulse reverberating in my ears. What was scaring me? Why was I so afraid? I'd sung our song a million times before, in the car and in the shower, on car rides up to wine country and alone in my cottage. My job required me to speak comfortably into a microphone, and as a speaker, a preacher, and a musician, I knew how to project my voice, how to speak words from my heart. But this moment was different, and perhaps the most intimate of all: I wasn't teaching or leading or directing other people. I was simply receiving the gift of love, complete with feelings of joy and heartache.

If loving this man meant saying yes to his pain, I would sing the song until my throat ran dry, until the words no longer came.

As I started to sing, though, a hiccup of surprise sprang from my father's mouth, a response to the melody or perhaps to the significance of the day. And it was as if the hiccup in his throat caught in my own throat seconds later, a perfection of sound interrupted by the strength of emotion. Still, I kept singing and I kept clinging to his arm as we walked around the trellis, behind the back row of chairs to the top of the center aisle, singing because I sing because I sing.[2] Soon all was quiet, a breath of silence as he and I walked down the aisle toward the man with tears streaming down his cheeks.

But then, joy. The holiest of joys, the deepest of sincerities.

James and I laughed and prayed and heeded Brian's instruction to fix our eyes on every person under the canopy of pines while Kaitlin and Bianca sang another song. I couldn't stop looking at James' father: leaning forward in his chair, he closed his eyes and lifted his hands toward the sky, a sacred overwhelm of love his alone to receive. His wife, Judy, sat beside him, eyes closed and mouth turned upward in a smile, tears falling down her face. I begged myself never to forget that moment, to sear its image in my memory. Of course, no sooner had one moment of sentiment passed and another begun did the faint scent of Sweet Baby Ray's Barbecue Sauce waft upward. The smell came not from the barrel drum roaster twenty yards away but from my own sweaty pores.

"The chicken!" I'd said aloud earlier that morning when I realized that no one had remembered to marinate it. *Damn do-it-yourself weddings,* I thought. I crept down the basement stairs in pajamas and flip-flops, and dumped packages of raw chicken and bottles of barbecue sauce into empty white painter's buckets. Soon my arms swam elbow-deep in poultry slime, sticky with the honeyed condiment. Twelve hours later, the scent remained. Who needed Chanel No. 5 when Eau de Volaille could be a bride's perfume of choice?

Despite my smelling like a chicken factory, James and I said our "I do's." And after Brian legally declared us wife and husband, by the power vested in him by the state of California, we danced our way down the aisle to awaiting glasses of champagne. We did as Jesus had taught us to do, eating and drinking and celebrating with the greatest company of saints. We gorged on a southern spread of barbecue chicken and steak, fried catfish, macaroni and cheese, cornbread and collard greens, and then later, after we'd passed the microphone to our fathers, on coconut cupcakes and red velvet cupcakes. Meanwhile, our hearts feasted on a most beloved gathering of family and friends, on the faces of those without whom we couldn't imagine sharing in the joys and tears of that day, and on watching our families mingle with one another, digging into the dance floor and swinging together on front-porch rocking chairs. Saying yes to one another and to a future unknown, we declared our union good.

*J*ames and I weren't the first interracial couple ever to meet, fall in love, and marry, but it also hasn't been that long in America's history that interracial couples have been allowed to marry. Less than half a century before we said "I do," the Supreme Court legalized interracial marriage in the United States when the power of one couple's love changed the American landscape.

Richard Loving, a white man, and Mildred Jeter, a mixed-race woman, met in the midfifties at a dance in rural Central Point, Virginia. They were six years apart in age. By the end of the decade, Jeter had dropped out of the eleventh grade, reportedly to birth and care for their first child. When the Lovings married in 1958, their interracial union wasn't the first in Central Point or in Caroline County, let alone in the rest of America.

At the time of the Lovings' vows, "only 4 percent of Americans approved of marriages between blacks and whites."[3] In 1958, the civil rights movement was still in its early years. Martin Luther King Jr. had been elected president of the Southern Christian Leadership Conference less than a year before, and prior to his delegation, Rosa Parks had refused to give up her seat on the bus, prompting the 355-day Montgomery Bus Boycott, sparking the movement into existence. Although the Supreme Court had unanimously voted in favor of school integration in *Brown v. Board of Education of Topeka* (1954), it was another three years before the Little Rock Nine walked through the doors of Central High School in Little Rock, Arkansas. But for many Americans, not just in the southern states but also across the country, there was a difference between supporting individual rights and allowing individuals of different races to intermix and marry.[4] It took something bigger and greater to break this mindset, something like a love as authentic and relatable as that of Richard and Mildred Loving.

When Mildred was eighteen and pregnant with their second child, the Lovings married in Washington, D.C., before moving back to Virginia to live with her parents. Five weeks later, three county sheriffs burst into their bedroom in the middle of the night. When one of the men asked what they were doing with each other, Mildred stated she was his wife. Richard pointed to the framed marriage certificate that hung over their bed (likely kept there in case the authorities tried to arrest them). According to Virginia's 1924 Racial Integrity Act, "all marriages between 'white' people and those who were 'colored'—meaning anyone 'with a drop of non-white blood,'"[5] were a felony. The two were carted off to separate rat-infested, out-dated jail cells, where Richard spent one day and Mildred spent five. (Some accounts state that she was held for the better part of a month.) When their case finally went to trial, local judge Leon Bazile urged them to "change their plea of not guilty to guilty and to go away qui-etly rather than challenge the law."[6] So they did. Instead of spending more time in jail, the two entered exile, forced to leave Virginia "at once and . . . not return together or at the same time . . . for a period of twenty-five years."[7]

The family of four moved to urban Washington, D.C., where they settled in with one of Mildred's cousins and eventually had a third child, a daughter. But as the old saying goes, you can take the girl out of the country, but you can't take the country out of the girl, and Mildred Loving yearned to return to the Virginia foothills. In 1963, five years after their arrest, she took matters into her own hands and penned a letter to Attorney General Robert Kennedy. Maybe he could help her family escape the cage of city life and return to the country.

Her effort reminds me of the story about a bleeding woman: if she could touch the hem of Jesus' garment, she'd be healed. Like her, Mary, the sister of dead Lazarus, also cried out, "Lord, if you had been here, my brother would not have died." Their cries are a chorus of *if only, if only, if only,* one after another after another. I don't doubt

Mildred Loving's cries were all that different: *If only I could get in touch with Bobby Kennedy, then we could return to Virginia. If only he would take our case, then we would be able to freely love one another as husband and wife.* She wasn't after fame. She wasn't trying to bolster the civil rights movement. She only wanted to return home.

And somehow her cries were heard. Within a month, the attorney general passed the letter on to the American Civil Liberties Union (ACLU), which took the case free of charge. Her lawyers[8] understood the fragile condition of racial relations in the United States, a tension not unlike our own today. Although Mildred was half Native American and half African American and tended to identify with her indigenous side, she still had dark skin—and the role Jim Crow had cast her in would need to be played up in order to "help dismantle a system that oppressed visibly dark people."[9] After four years, the case arrived to the highest court in the land, where all nine judges unanimously overturned the decision against the Lovings, reversing antimiscegenation laws everywhere.[10]

I think about what it must have been like to be in the courtroom that day, to stand in the middle of uproarious shouts of victory and gasps of horror, to witness a court ruling that changed the direction of a nation. James and I wouldn't think twice about the legality of our marriage when we stood under the pines nearly forty-five years later. But in the late sixties, it must have been equal parts magical and maddening that something as simple as love should be determined by outward appearances, that the institution of marriage should take so long to redeem.

*S*ometimes I wondered how much James and I really shared with the Lovings, though. They lived in the South, where white racists wore their affiliations like a badge of honor. We lived on the

West Coast in a city that supposedly checked prejudice at the door, the eradication of racism a value of progressive society. Despite my naivete about the place we lived, I wasn't unaware of our different skin colors, of his African American ancestry and my European American roots. But in a way, my love for James ran only skin deep, and my understanding of his story, particularly when it came to race, was surface level. Although I had peeled back a layer or two of the onion—mostly of his story and of his father's story—it took much longer to reach the heart of the matter. Meanwhile, our contrasting skin colors were sometimes a thing of exoticism to me, something that made us different and special, something that set us apart from our friends and from most of the people in our neighborhood.

So I laughed when in Hawaii for our honeymoon, James slathered more sunscreen on his body than I did. "Oh, love, I'm the one who gets sunburned," I'd say, pointing to my pale, freckled skin and chuckling at his silly antics as he ran his hand in circles over his bald head, on down to his legs, his ankles, his toes.

And on Sunday mornings, when we drove down Cesar Chavez, took a left onto Dolores, and strolled through the front doors of our church, I didn't give much thought to a sanctuary filled with folks who looked mostly like me. These were our people, our friends, our community; as one of the only black men in that building, James added a particular flavor to the place, his presence all the mission statement needed to claim a multicultural presence in the city of San Francisco.

And when on Friday and Saturday nights we took the train downtown for sushi and a movie, I'd glance at our reflection in store windows, enamored by how we somehow stood out from other couples and blended together, all at the same time. Looking at him, I felt equal parts longing and desire not only for who he was as a person but also for who he was as someone who was different from me. "See him, see this, see us?" I wanted to say to couples passing by, as if he was a prize to show off, a novelty to carry with me like a small dog in a sparkly silver tote. It was like I'd forgotten why the Lovings had to fight for their marriage in the first place.

Whether or not a tendency to show off comes with newlywed territory, I still had a long way to go when it came to understanding our ethnic, cultural, and racial differences. Unlike the Lovings, we didn't need to hang our marriage certificate above the headboard, nor did we have to fight tooth and nail to get the state of California to recognize our marriage as sacred and holy. But perhaps like Mildred and Richard Loving, there existed within me complications I hadn't yet come to understand about interracial marriage, complications I would continue to navigate for the rest of my life.

I wanted to believe our love for each other was enough, just as I wanted who we were on the outside to be enough for the rest of the world. But before that could happen, we had to survive the first couple of years of marriage, differences and all.

CHAPTER 7

Differences

One night, James and I gathered with three couples around our dining room table for an evening of intentionality in friendship with one another. We would meet together weekly, we pledged. We would eat good food and share a glass of wine and get real with one another. Even though our group stemmed from church, we promised not to dissect the week's sermon or answer any prefabricated questions designed to promote discussion. Instead, we would listen for the real and true stories of our lives. We would be each other's people.

"What's something you didn't know about your spouse before you got married?" David prompted as the rest of us crowded around the table, huddling over steaming bowls of chicken tortilla soup topped with chips and avocado and cheese.

"How Cara wants to recycle everything in sight!" James said.

"How James wants to keep every piece of paper that's ever crossed his path!" I replied, prompting a shrug from my husband before he gently squeezed my thigh in affirmation. It was true: when my overzealousness to reduce, reuse, and recycle met his penchant to print off and save every card, bill, and letter, it was nothing but trouble for our young marriage. Still, we chose laughter, between the two of us and in the whole group, and from that night on, a combina-tion of joy and honesty became the thread of our evenings together.

At one point, I looked at the faces gathered around the table: our group looked different from those who usually joined us for dinner. I tended to line up our weekly calendar, so if we were having people over, it was because I had invited them to join us. Except for some of the adults and students I worked with in ministry, most of the time I invited my friends and the people in my circles to join us—and almost all of those people were white.

But that night, James wasn't the only person of color: a Latino couple, a black couple, and a white couple sat around our table. The eight of us talked in earnest about the good things and hard things of being newly married, about the loneliness that sometimes comes with marriage: You feel all alone even when your partner sits two feet away from you. You mourn the loss of friendship when "his" friends and "her" friends don't morph into "our" friends.

As the night went on, a funny thing happened: those of us who were white took a back seat in conversation, the majority for once becoming the minority. I sat back in my chair, observing the cama-raderie of my husband and our friends, feeling like I didn't belong, like I wasn't included.

I didn't get their jokes about government cheese, but I laughed anyway.

I couldn't comprehend how stories that seemed sad and hard to swallow, stories about being the only dark-skinned person in a sea of white faces, resulted in a laugh-so-hard-you-cry kind of laughter. How was exclusion, in any way, shape, or form, even remotely funny?

And I didn't understand how, more than a year into marriage, James seemed to have instantaneous solidarity with a table full of strangers, coming alive with them more than he ever had in two years with my friends.

*T*here are a number of ways to interpret the scene in our dining room that night. Sociologists and psychologists often lean into the phrase "double consciousness," which was coined by W. E. B. DuBois. Because blacks (and other ethnic minority groups) were "simultaneously 'inside and outside the West,' . . . minorities develop two senses of self, one derived from their daily perceptions and experiences within their respective communities and another *internalized* sense of self derived from the perceptions, dominant expectations, and Euro-intellectual tradition of the dominant society."[1] Because of this double consciousness, there really *was* a distinct difference in the way James interacted with our friends of color around the table that night. My husband didn't have to acquiesce to the perceptions and expectations of dominant culture, but he was free to be his truest, most unedited self.

Theologians and philosophers, on the other hand, often call it a commonality of oppression. If I were to dust off an old book from seminary, I'd remember that in liberation theology, the eyes of culture always count, for the oppressed are always on the lookout for a redeemer, a liberator, a savior of spirits and souls.[2] As we ate together that night, soup dribbling down our chins, the stories that rang solely of injustice to me became a common, binding experience for those who shared their pain aloud. The "I" became the "we," the tangled roots of oppression and injustice the very stuff of shared experience.

As a white woman who lives and breathes a predominantly white existence, I have never—nor will I ever—experienced oppression, at least not because of the color of my skin. I might see the effects of racial oppression firsthand because my life is intertwined with a man who has fought against the grave realities of injustice, but I will never fully experience what it means to be slighted for having darker skin.

I will never be forced to adapt to a culture that is not my own, for mine is the dominant culture. Mine is the culture to which others are expected to adapt. Until that evening's dinner, I held the upper hand, mine "the unfair privilege of majority peoples to not worry about the difference ethnicity makes; it is not an important part of [their] everyday lives."[3] But that night, when the tides of conversation turned, an essential element of liberation theology began to float within me.

My mind swam with questions when I lay in bed at night and as James and I continued to meet with that table of friends. Charmed by our marriage, I'd naively looked at the two of us and believed we were above it all. Ours was the kind of love Paul McCartney and Stevie Wonder sang into their microphones, a bond more substantial than that of a piano's black and white keys. I somehow believed our relationship plumbed the depths of racial harmony, transcending race and class, culture and education, the integration of our lives the only evidence necessary for the naysayers. So I adopted the tune as our own, dedicating it to him with a group of girlfriends during a night of karaoke in Chinatown and endlessly singing it in the shower afterward.

"Let's make this our official first dance, love!" I said to James when we were in the early stages of planning our wedding.

"Yeah, I don't know about that," he replied.

"But it's our song, it's us: you're the ebony, I'm the ivory!"

"I understand that. But it's not even a dance song. It's not even in the top five hundred dance songs, so why would we dance to it at our wedding?"

I let out a groan.

"Ugh. You're so practical," I finally said, kissing him on the cheek as I imagined his suave ebony self gracing the dance floor, twirling and delighting in me, his ivory bride.

A shared faith, a sense of humor, and an attraction to each other had been our glue. Everything else we dismissed as unimportant at worst and secondary at best. Sure, we didn't see eye to eye on everything, but we were on the same page when it came to the most important elements of a relationship: religion, finances, children, and quality of life. Our skin color had simply been the icing on top, and in my postracial understanding of the world, our racial identities hadn't mattered in the least. Instead, it had only served to make *us* that much more charming, interesting, and distinguishable from everyone else.

*B*ut the question kept coming up.

"Is it hard being in an interracial relationship?" our friends Holly and Andrew asked us over freshly poured cups of Philz coffee in San Francisco's Mission Bay neighborhood. Their curiosity was genuine. Andrew held up a copy of *Divided by Faith,* a book that sought to prove how eleven o'clock on a Sunday morning was still the most racially divided time in America. Passionate about conversations of race and justice, he and Holly had devoured the book, and now, sitting across from us, they wanted to know if the truth applied to us as well.

"Nah," we quickly replied, our responses almost singsong in nature. We always claimed it'd be different if we lived in the South or in the Pacific Northwest, where we spent our formative years. But those weren't the places we had chosen to live and lay down our roots as adults. There, people did gaze at us; there, people did wonder. When we visited Oregon, the good church people stared at the lone black man in a sea of six hundred white bodies. "Why, hello! And who do we have here?" they'd say, always with kindness and always good naturedly, not realizing how wide their eyes had grown when they shook his hand, how transfixed they were when James said a simple hello.

And when we visited Mississippi, the good people of Aunt Jessica's church stared at the white woman alone in a sea of four hundred black faces.

"And do we have any visitors in the house today?" the minister bellowed from the front stage, looking directly at me. One of his hands shook with the power of the Holy Spirit while the other beckoned me to stand. Twisting my arms from the backs of the chairs beside me, where my nieces sat, I stood slowly, acutely aware of the sweat trickling down my back, of my cheeks flaming red with embarrassment.

"James," I whispered, "you're a visitor too!"

"Oh, yeah. Almost forgot," he replied, a lopsided grin stretching across his face. The two of us stood to their applause, fingertips touching over the girls' heads, eager for the moment to pass.

And we felt this contrast when we hopped on an airplane and flew away from the San Francisco Bay Area, the stark reality of the places we once called home sometimes too hard for the other person to swallow. But apart from the church and from the places we tended to visit more than call home, we questioned whether we felt the tension of being in an interracial relationship in California too.

Like clockwork, we stopped and paused and nodded our heads.

"You go first, love," I said softly, and James began talking not about Sunday mornings but about the two of us.

"I love my wife so much," he began, "but sometimes we're so different. And sometimes, she doesn't always realize those differences come from our different experiences of race." I nodded. When we clashed, I tended to believe it was because he was male, I was female. He was left-brained, I was right-brained. He was introverted, I was extroverted. I didn't see our differences through a lens of racial understanding, let alone through the differences of ethnicity or culture. I saw our differences solely through a lens of personality and of how we related to other people.[4]

I'd heard him tell the story a hundred times about "growing up black in Mississippi," but I hadn't really understood what that phrase meant to him. I hadn't understood how the negative words and stereotypes spoken over him at such a young age would continue to make a home in his soul, how those same feelings of shame and inferiority would become the broken record of his story. Because this repeated song of brokenness ran so deeply within him, it would fight for a place in our marriage and rally for a seat at the table. Just as I had been told I could be anything I wanted to be when I grew up, as long as I tried hard enough and gave it my all, he had been told he would never amount to much of anything. He had been labeled ignorant, stupid, inferior. "Descendent of Ham!" "Child of the apes!" "Boy!" they called him, unaware of the impact of their words, ignorant of how he would walk away feeling unloved and unwelcomed by society, all because he'd been born a black boy in the South.

"But then I found God," James said, his eyes filling with tears.

"Or maybe God found you," I added.

James nodded. "Or maybe God found me—that too. I found answers in the living Word of God, in the one who called me his own. And that's when I understood it was all a lie. Their words, their names, their beliefs about me: all a lie."

The four of us sat in silence for a few moments, absorbing the weight of his story.

"But just because you now realize it was all a lie," I said softly, "doesn't mean those words don't still find a way into our marriage." I paused, glancing at James for permission to continue. "So, yeah, sometimes it's hard being in an interracial marriage, hard in ways we're only just now realizing, hard in ways we won't fully realize for another ten, twenty, thirty years."

"But that doesn't mean you're not trying?" Holly asked.

"That doesn't mean we're not trying," I replied, acutely aware of the many layers of our relationship and of how I still sometimes wanted to run from all of the pain. I had chosen to love him. I had chosen to move forward in our relationship and then in marriage, saying a hearty yes to James, till death do us part. And through this act, his pain had become my pain, the racism poured over him a wound now seared onto my soul.

*A*t the time we married, interracial couples made up nearly a quarter of all new marriages in California and nearly a tenth of marriages in the United States.[5] In a sense, James and I fit the mold of those likely to leap over racial lines in marriage: we were on the younger end of the age spectrum, we lived in an urban area, and we were both college educated. But that didn't mean we had arrived.

"You're brave to choose an interracial marriage," a therapist told me.

"I'm sorry, what? Brave? Surely this has nothing to do with bravery," I replied. "This has everything to do with falling in love and marrying a man whose skin happens to be darker than my own." I looked at her and glared. Her words were not helpful in that moment, not for my heart and certainly not for my marriage.

"It takes bravery to admit the differences of your respective experiences and stories, especially when it comes to issues of race and ethnicity. And it takes bravery to face those differences head on, especially in a marriage."

I stared again, first at her and then out the window to my left, wondering whether she was right, wondering whether my marriage had required a certain amount of bravery I hadn't ever taken the time to wrap my mind around. Was it bravery or a naive unwillingness to admit what facing our differences might really mean?

One night when James was stuck late at the office, I couldn't get the therapist's words out of my head. I curled up on the couch, laptop to my right, pen and notepad to my left, Mr. Darcy at my feet. I would figure this problem out. On the one hand, regardless of whether I believed race played a role in our relationship, statistics surrounding interracial marriage in the US still supported the naysayers. One study said that "14 percent of whites, Hispanics and Asians polled said they would oppose such a marriage."[6] Even though that number was down from 63 percent in 1990, another study from less than fifteen years before found that 10 percent of whites and 5 percent of blacks "were in favor of a law banning marriage between blacks and whites."[7] I sat there wondering what I was supposed to do with all of this information, especially when the negative seemed to overwhelm the positive. I wanted to clothe my body in bravery, but I also wondered how to dress in garments of steel when it seemed like we could never win the war, when it felt like my enemies always lurked around the next corner. And all of this said nothing of the 24 percent of African American men who married someone of a different race or ethnicity,[8] a reality one of my African American girlfriends later described to me as the worst kind of betrayal.

Staring at the screen in front of me, I shrugged and raised my hands in the air. I give up. I give in. I bow to the numbers. I believe they might have something to tell me.

Call me brave.

Call me an anomaly.

And call me oblivious to challenges and situations I wouldn't necessarily have embraced had I married someone who identified as white.

But one thing was true: James' devotion had saved me and changed me and grown me in ways I was just beginning to understand. Even if our relationship came with its own set of differences,

I could tune my ears to listen, maybe for the first time. I could open my eyes to see the things I hadn't yet seen and didn't yet know, the underpinnings of my story and my past, something that would take a lifetime to understand.

And maybe when this happened, I would also see that justice and wholeness were mine to bathe and swim in and be cleansed by as well.

CHAPTER 8

Black Santa

It was our first Christmas together as a married couple, and I couldn't wait for James to experience some of the traditions of my childhood. We flew north from San Francisco to Portland, no sooner arriving on the tarmac before the enveloping arms of my parents accosted us with festivity and joy, their excitement palpable and contagious. After we'd thrown our bags onto the floor of my high school bedroom, we loaded into the car again, this time on our way to a Christmas tree farm to chop down a tree.

"Don't people get paid to do this?" James asked after my sister and I discovered the perfect tree, a Douglas fir that rendered him prostrate on the ground, a handsaw in one fist, and pine needles and dirt in the other.

"Yeah, but it's so much more *fun* to pick out your own tree," I quipped, adding in a bit about this being his rite of passage as the newest married man in the MacDonald family. I may have believed myself an egalitarian, but when it came to chopping down Christmas trees, I deferred to the power of the patriarchy and to my husband's strong forearms.

"Well, I vote that the guy in the grocery store parking lot does it for us next year," he said, wiping sweat off his brow just as I blew him a kiss. We loaded the tree on top of the car, drove it home, and dragged it into the house, cramming thirty-year-old ornaments onto its sagging branches as we sang along to Nat King Cole tunes and clinked mugs of hot buttered rum. Over the next four days, James and I took a deep dive into the only version of Christmas I'd ever known, of food and family, of gift giving and late-night card playing and a hushed Christmas Eve service lit by candles.

But I soon learned that the story of an old white man coming down our chimney would never be part of our traditions and our story, not if James had any say in it.

A night or two after we arrived, James and I strolled down Peacock Lane, a four-block street in Southeast Portland famous for holiday lights and decorations. My best friend, Mindy, and her husband lived less than a block away from this iconic location with their infant son. We wanted to grab a couple of hours of quality time together, so taking a walk up and down the lane made sense.

The place was hopping, treelined sidewalks packed with families eager to see the middling show, the streets bumper to bumper with cars full of rabid fans. Mindy, the queen of conversation, didn't waste any time asking James a question she'd asked others a thousand times before, its answer revelatory to her understanding of a person's parents, home, and level of Americanism versus religiosity.

"So, James, did you grow up believing in Santa Claus?"

My husband threw his head back and laughed, his response a guffaw, the deepest, heartiest kind of belly laugh.

"Santa Claus? *Santa Claus?* No, I did not grow up believing in Santa Claus," he finally said, wiping tears from his eyes. His tone was loud and defiant, different from anything Mindy had ever heard him use before. Still, she dug in.

"Tell me more about that," she replied. "Did your parents just not celebrate that tradition? Mine didn't, and I'm always curious to hear how families address their belief in Santa."

James looked at her, at her husband, and at me, his eyes searching for some kind of understanding. The fields of Mississippi took root in his voice.

"Where I grew up, ain't no white man coming down your chimney bringing you gifts! I didn't believe in that kind of Santa Claus, and neither did the people I knew: we *couldn't* believe in notions of a white man sliding down a chimney in the middle of the night to bring you a bag full of gifts, because the whole idea was impossible. It didn't make any sense! What else can I say? Santa's not real!" He was practically shouting at that point, his voice deep, southern, black.

I shushed him. I wasn't embarrassed by his thoughts or opinions—Old Saint Nick hadn't been a deal breaker in our relationship. But I was embarrassed by his lack of sensitivity to the people around us. Undeterred by their stares, he hadn't quieted down when the man in front of us clamped his hands over his daughter's ears or when the woman to our right turned and whispered, "Are you kidding me?" He hadn't cared what they thought of him. He hadn't cared how it made us look.

"James," Mindy said, "you mean because you're black, there was an impossibility of a white man ever coming down your chimney to bring you gifts? Like, of course, that whole idea never happened and would never happen? And not just in your house but in anybody's house? This wasn't ever happening not because reindeer can't fly but because you're black? And *this* is why Santa never existed for you?" Her questions came as a point of clarification, mostly for her, maybe for the rest of us.

James nodded vigorously, the vehemence of his answer completed by a wild exclamation of hands. "Yes! If there was an old white man coming down your chimney, something was *wrong*. You'd better run for your life! He's not bringin' you no gifts!"

Mindy and I would circle back to that conversation over the years, for that night was the start of something in her and in me too. Of it, she later wrote, "The knowing was so deep for him. It was in his bones. In his blood. It could not part from him. He did not have the advantage to forget what it meant to be black, so he laughed out of spite. He laughed at my whiteness. He laughed that—on this street full of lights and hope and American dreams about Christmas and redemption and getting gifts from God or Santa or whomever— there were still people like me (read: educated, white, liberal) who had no idea of the implications of four hundred years of systemic racism in America." James and I would return to that night too, to a time when I hadn't yet grasped how deep the hurt ran, when I cared more about the reactions of strangers than my husband's pain in the dazzle and glitter of holiday lights.

*P*erhaps like many Americans, I tend to romanticize my past. I think about Santa Claus and Baby Jesus and the Christmas season, and my mind focuses on the sparkly parts. I remember how candy canes taste best in December, how crab and butter taste best on Christmas Eve. I yearn for the haunting melodies of "O Holy Night" and "O Come, O Come, Emmanuel," and I remember as idyllic the weeks off from school, the afternoons spent holed up reading a book, a cup of hot chocolate in the crook of a blanket. Oftentimes my memory retains snapshots only of the good, leaving no room for the bad, not for myself and not for others. But what of those truths I tend to gloss and skip over?

I think about sitting on the back porch of a cabin at camp one summer, legs dangling over the railing next to a shy high school girl.

I watched silently, almost helplessly, as tears rolled down her cheeks. There was nothing I could say to take away the pain of losing her father to cancer, no wand I could wave to erase her memory of discovering him cold in his bed. I could only put my arms around her and draw her toward me, and even that didn't feel like enough. In a moment like the one she and I shared under the stars, if I'm truly listening, then the stories of another person's life hold a certain power to change me, and the rosy pictures of my past take on a different hue. Old Saint Nick doesn't look so red and jolly and merry, and when I read real accounts of American history, the flags of my state and of my country don't fly so high and bright and untarnished anymore either.

Growing up in Oregon, my generation watched archaic 1970s filmstrips and made scrappy art projects of twigs from our back yards and cotton balls from our mamas' bathrooms. But we also staked a claim to The Oregon Trail, the only game we could play on the lone computer in the back of the classroom. When I made good choices at school, I got to put giant earphones over my ears and hunt for rabbits and squirrels and bison. I got to honor every grainy, computerized family member who died along the route with a legitimate funeral and burial rites. And I got to put my church-girl prayers to use.

"Dear God, please, please, please don't let anyone die as we cross over the Snake River today," I'd whisper, aware of the division of church and state.

"Dear heavenly Father, please don't let uncontrollable nineteenth-century diseases be the end of our two-thousand-mile journey. In your name I pray, amen," I'd add, whispering another amen or two to seal the deal. Really, I just wanted my covered wagon and as many dysentery-free family members as possible to arrive in the Oregon Territory, in the lush and fertile place I called home.

Perhaps like many ten-year-old children, I felt a certain amount of pride in my home state: like the pioneers on the computer screen, my parents had also crossed rivers and mountains (albeit on a major interstate and over several bridges) to find home. I may have complained about the weather, but I still considered Oregon the greatest state of all. To this place, my classmates and I raised sticky hands in salutation, paying homage to the men and women of our history books who put the Pacific Northwest on the map. *To them! To us! To our state!*

But in the fourth grade, we didn't learn about Oregon's unique history of racism, the first (and only) state admitted to the union with an exclusion clause written into its constitution. Throughout the 1840s and '50s, growing numbers of white settlers left their homes in the Midwest, South, and East to head west, bringing with them their ideals, experiences, and histories of hurt. Although many emigrants vehemently opposed slavery, they also opposed living alongside African Americans. They opposed the prospect of losing jobs and wages, because "many were non-slaveholding farmers from Missouri and other border states who had struggled to compete against those who owned slaves."[1] These early settlers established a white mecca, and by the time Oregon became a state on February 14, 1859, it was illegal for persons of color to enter it.

In 1843, a small population of settlers unanimously declared Oregon a free state, written as a provision of the 1787 Northwest Ordinance: "There shall be neither slavery nor involuntary servitude in the said territory otherwise than in the punishment of crimes whereof the party shall have been duly convicted."[2] To my ten-year-old self, this is where the conversation both began and ended: because Oregon, from its inception, declared itself free from the institution of slavery, racism didn't exist where we lived. And if racism didn't exist, then there was no way we could be a racist people.

The war between the North and the South, between the Union

states and those of the Confederacy, was fought between those who opposed slavery and those who were for slavery. But it also centered on trade, tariffs, and states' rights, the latter being the real reason why the state of Mississippi fought against my father-in-law's integration nearly one hundred years later. Mississippi wanted to retain its rights as an individual state, including the right to decide whether its schools should be integrated. Under the leadership of Ross Barnett, the state was willing to pit itself against the US government, running roughshod over a single man who just wanted to get the education he deserved, in order to get its way.

And was my home state any different?

Although Oregon's involvement in the war was minimal, she had always worked to establish her rights as an individual state, further digging into ideals of whiteness. In 1844, less than a year after declaring Oregon a free state,[3] Oregon's provisional council, led by a Missourian named Peter Burnett,[4] gave slaveholders a three-year grace period to remove slave property. So slavery became legal in my home state for the next three years.[5] But the clause didn't stop there: once they became free, former slaves were no longer allowed to reside in the territory. Women had to leave the state within three years, men within two, and if the freed chose to stay, they were subject to the Lash Law. Burnett threatened thirty-nine lashes, repeated every six months, for anyone who overstayed his or her welcome.[6] Thirty-nine, the same number of lashes Jesus received before dying on the cross, one lash short of death, theologians say.

Although voters rescinded the law within a year, I can imagine Burnett standing on a wooden platform under the same drizzly gray skies I once stood under: "The object is to keep clear of that most troublesome class of population [blacks]. We are in a new world, under the most favorable circumstances and we wish to avoid most of those evils that have so much afflicted the United States and other countries."[7] No lashings were ever recorded, but a precedent of fear was established that day, the long holdings of white supremacy rooted in the land.

In 1849, three years after the Lash Law was repealed, the provisional legislature enacted a second law specifying it was unlawful for any "negro or mulatto" to enter or live in the Oregon Territory.[8] Just as Oregonians feared job losses, they feared black seamen who might jump ship and team up with native populations, fomenting hostility toward white people—after all, we fear that which we do not know, and free former slaves were something white residents did not know. Although the law was rescinded five years later,[9] it didn't stop the state from writing one final exclusion clause into the state constitution, a law that prohibited anyone of African American descent from coming into, residing in, or being within the state's borders.[10]

I think about the "Keep Out!" signs I used to tape onto my bedroom door and onto the trapdoor of the tree house in our back yard. My ten-year-old self wanted a space to call her own, free from the annoyances of my siblings before joining hands at the table and snuggling on the couch to listen as Dad read a chapter from *Tom Sawyer*. I like to think the signs remained only until the tape lost its stickiness or until Mom kindly reminded me of the Golden Rule. But when I think about my home state, although it was established as free, it was not established as free for every person, at least not for every person with black or brown skin. Instead, according to Winston Grady-Willis, director of the School of Gender, Race and Nations at Portland State University, "Oregon is the only state in the United States that actually began as literally whites-only. Even though there was subsequent legislation that challenged those statutes, the statutes were not removed from the books until 1922."[11] And sixty-six years is longer than sticky tape should last, longer than a sign ever should have hung.

When I read about the exclusion laws for the first time, a reading that didn't happen until well into my twenties, I experienced something like the stages of grief. Shocked, at first I didn't believe it was true. But then I kept digging, and as I put my shovel into the ground, anger came with it. "Take that!" I wanted to shout to my state's ancestors, before I bargained never to do the same as they had, and before I entered a period of loss and sadness over that which I could not change. But then, acceptance: I admitted that Oregon is in me and I am in it, that the laws written on her walls before I even came into being are a part of me, just as I am a part of her. I recognized my complicity, knowing that it took both of us far too long to learn from our mistakes.

For that wasn't the only exclusion that took too long to remove. After the Civil War, Oregon refused to approve the Fourteenth and Fifteenth Amendments of the US Constitution. The Fourteenth Amendment, which passed in 1866 and was ratified in 1868, granted citizenship to "all persons born or naturalized in the United States,"[12] including former slaves. According to a 2017 article in the *Washington Post,* Oregon did not adopt the Fourteenth Amendment into its constitution until 1973, perhaps then conscious of its mistake.[13] The Fifteenth Amendment, which passed in 1869 and was ratified in 1870, granted black men the right to vote. Oregon did not approve this change until 1959, exactly one hundred years after it became a state, a symbolic adoption at its centennial celebration. Had we realized our blunders by then, the depth of our guilt and shame?

Even if Oregonians eventually repealed exclusion laws, and even if the state government eventually chose to adopt the laws of the nation, it was too late. Oregon had been established as a place by whites and for whites. Word spread among the African American community following the Civil War, during the Jim Crow era, and even during the Great Migration, when more than five million blacks left the South for the North and the West: you're not welcome here.[14] But one group of folks found a home in Oregon: by the early 1920s, the Ku Klux Klan had successfully established the largest chapter west of the Mississippi River. And to me, that said it all.

*N*early a decade after James and I took a walk down Peacock Lane that drizzly December night, I sat with Mindy on her sloping front lawn in Southeast Portland. Burgers and a tossed salad, carrots and celery sticks and crinkly potato chips, water and white wine dotted the picnic blanket where we lazed, sipping our drinks and savoring our food. I think she and I both hoped time would slow down just long enough for us to remember the smell of the grass, the taste of the moment.

"Hey, Charles!" Mindy called, inviting her neighbor and his infant son over to join us. The two of them saw each other nearly every day, the intersection of their lives as common an occurrence as the two cups of coffee I religiously drink every morning.

"Nice to meet you," he drawled, his voice thick and southern, so different from the accents I was used to hearing on this side of the country. Soon we got to chatting about his work as a doctor in a VA hospital and about the differences between the Deep South and the Pacific Northwest.

"You know, it's interesting," he finally said, pausing. "The thing about race in the South is that people aren't afraid to say what they really think. If they're racist, they're racist and proud of it. They wear it like a flag, you know? But in the Northwest, it's a different story. It's like it's in the water, but no one wants to admit they're drinking it."

I nodded slowly: is this what it meant to grow up in this place, to not even know what was in the water I drank? When a place is rooted in systemic racism, the effects of laws enacted to keep communities safe, protect the working class's jobs, and fulfill the American dream trickle down from generation to generation in ways that favor some and not all. Certain ways of thinking filter into education and politics and religion, and we drink the water, not knowing it comes from lily-white wells. Try as we might, we are not protected from the water we drink.

But then, we do know. We know and we are changed by the stories we hear, by the accounts we read, by the tales we absorb. So if the hurt is still present, what is the role of remembrance, of paying homage to the truth of yesterday?

In "Facing Our Legacy of Lynching," a cover story for *Christianity Today*, D. L. Mayfield writes about stumbling upon the story of Alonzo Tucker, a black man from Coos Bay, Oregon, who was lynched in 1902 after being accused of assaulting a white woman. Mayfield attempts to honor Tucker's life with a small memorial at the site, then investigates the history of lynching in the United States and discovers an effort in Alabama to memorialize the more than four thousand African Americans lynched in the US between 1877 through the early 1950s. She muses over what it means to remember and what it means to discard, especially when it comes to those stories that aren't so neatly wrapped up in a bow. "For Christians, that is also a key function of the Bible—a collection of memories, divinely breathed to be passed down through traditions and communities. So many of the stories, especially in the Old Testament, are not cut-and-dried morality tales or inspirational anecdotes. They are portraits of people who were wrestling with loving God and loving their neighbors, and they are full of both cautionary notes and urgings to be more faithful and righteous. Remember God's covenants; remember God's commandments."[15]

In my tendency to romanticize, I can gloss over entire sections in the Bible, especially if they're not shiny and pretty, if they don't leave a good taste in my mouth. I can open to Psalm 139, a song by David about the God who searched him and knew him, about the one who knit him together in his mother's womb. My heart swells within me, growing bigger with each verse, but then I stop. My eyes squint against the abrupt change of message, nineteen verses in: "If only you, God, would slay the wicked! / Away from me, you who are bloodthirsty!"[16] David continues to speak, to shout, to accuse his enemies, hating those who hate his Lord, counting them his foes. I shut the pages of the holy book and close my eyes: this is not what I want to remember, this is what I want to discard.

But with this story, as with every story, I do not get to choose which pieces I will keep. Instead, I take, I gather, I collect it all. I build an altar of words. I honor forgotten dignities lost along the way. I hold their pain as my own.

CHAPTER 9

Learning to Listen

As the months and years went by, James and I settled into the rhythms of marriage, into a syncopation of connecting at nighttime and on the weekends. We lived for these moments, for shared meals and lazy nights of snuggling on the couch, for the quiet ease with which we moved around each other and in our space. He worked a high-powered job in finance, and I worked a demanding around-the-clock job in ministry. I loved the work I got to do, especially when, in the midst of fundraising, budgetary analysis, and volunteer recruitment, I got to share a cup of coffee with an adult volunteer or treat a high school student to a smoothie. There was nothing greater in my book than those unexpected moments of solidarity, one human with another, when I had the pleasure of simply being a friend to someone.

More often than not, those conversations nestled into my soul, each sentence changing me for the better and somehow finding a way into my marriage too. Because I spent more hours at my job than with my husband, the different parts and people of my work became parts of James' life as well. Even though he didn't work with the students and adult volunteers very often, their stories still found a way into his heart.

And eventually, those stories changed both of us.

Keisa had been a regular in our Monday night program for a couple of years, and she also held a standing date in my calendar every Wednesday afternoon. The scene was usually the same. Pick her up from school. Grab a smoothie or coffee frappe. Head somewhere around San Mateo, find a spot to chill and hang out for an hour or so. Talk about God and boys and high school. Gab about her identity as a first-generation Tongan, about being part of the Peninsula's tightly knit Polynesian community. I thought we'd talked about everything, but then one day she uttered a sentence that changed it all, a conversation that James and I would rehash for years afterward.

"I don't like white people," she said bluntly. Her statement seemed to come out of nowhere, the candor of the accusation not lost on me.

"Um, Keisa, you do realize I'm white, don't you?" I didn't know what to say, so I said the only thing I could think of: a quippy and slightly sassy reply, one I hoped would curb the conversation so I wouldn't have to discover my role in it. Surely this didn't apply to me. Did it?

She strummed her ukulele absentmindedly, the tune behind her fingers the background music to words that would hum over me for the rest of my life. Her eyes filled with tears.

"You're different. You don't count," she murmured, staring at the sidewalk in front of her, her answer consolation for a truth I wasn't ready to hear. You could hear a deep sorrow coming from her throat; tears cascaded down her face as her fingers kept strumming a C chord, an E chord, an A chord, a progression she repeated again and again. She spoke the only stories she had ever known, of white people who threatened to take away her family's house, of white employees who followed her around their stores, of white teachers who wouldn't listen to her, who were always telling her what to do.

"White people don't listen and they don't care!" she finally said, my ears a witness to this indictment of the people who took one look at the color of her skin and labeled her stupid, lazy, a criminal. "They just think I'm dumb and fat."

"Oh, friend, that is not who you are, not in the least," I replied, wrapping my arms around her as she cried on my chest. My mouth whispered a thousand "I'm sorry's," unsure how to respond or what to say.

I wanted my words to fix the situation and take away the pain inside of her. I wanted the ministry I was part of and the God who loved her more than anything else to be enough to bind up her brokenness. I wanted to erase the wounds of racism and hate, but this wasn't about the white lady with good and moral intentions swooping in to save a brown girl's experiences of racism and hate.

A change had taken root deep inside of me. But it was a change bound by a force greater than ourselves, a liberation that could happen only if the two of us chose to walk the path together.

*O*h, love," I told James that night, "I just want to learn how to listen, how to listen for those things I haven't cared enough to listen for before." Even though Keisa had told me I was different, I knew that I was complicit. I wasn't exempt from her beliefs about white people. Now, more than ever, I wanted to listen for the sounds and the stories I hadn't listened for before. I wanted to tune my ears to hear a new song.

"Well, I look forward to hearing what your listening ears have to hear," he finally said, a knowing smile spread across his face.

James, of course, knew what would happen: I would listen intently, and with the enthusiasm of a four-year-old given strict orders to eat every piece of candy in my Halloween bag on a single night,

I would engorge myself with everything my mind and ears and eyes were hearing and seeing. Ever the faithful husband, he would listen to my sugar-induced rant, shielding himself from the force of my enthusiasm when the positive result of his listening caused me to bounce excitedly from one end of the room to another.

After all, some of us are born with a knack for listening, heeding the advice of our parents and teachers to listen before we speak. As children, we knew the world didn't need another sounding gong, so we became Peer Helpers in middle school, therapists and psychologists as grown-ups. I knew a listener lived somewhere inside of me, but she was crammed behind a dusty burgundy Esprit bag, forgotten New Kids on the Block paraphernalia, and a neon pink Caboodle filled with purple eyeshadow and Revlon's Toast of New York lipstick. Because I was a shy child, my cheeks flamed red with embarrassment whenever a teacher called on me. I didn't want to say the wrong thing, and I didn't want my body to betray me, so I held back even when I knew the answer. But in holding back, the listener within me grew, becoming what Mark Twain calls a natural noticer, an observer of the world, a listener for things not seen.

When I started wearing contacts for the first time in the seventh grade, though, I wasn't so scared anymore. And when, primed by a summer of swimming, I shot up five inches in less than three months and lost all of my baby fat, I didn't feel so self-conscious. I entered middle school with an unprecedented amount of confidence, unafraid to speak up and voice my opinion. Instead of my being the listener, people listened to me. They respected me and revered me and handed me awards as I danced across the stage and took it all in. I gulped down the glory, believing in a mantra that I could do and be anything I wanted.

Now, nearly twenty years later, I was ready to be a listener again.

"Before you do anything at all in your new job," an old supervisor had once said to me, "just listen. Don't bring any sudden changes to the place but just get to know the culture. Listen to it. Become a learner of the people and the places around you. Just listen." His advice had to do with a culture of ministry, but when it came to conversations of racial justice and liberation, if I wanted to learn how to walk on the path with people, I had to learn how to listen first.

*A*s I thought more about my conversation with Keisa, I also wondered about the intricately woven threads of Christianity and whiteness, of a religion and a Jesus I tended to believe looked just like me. Had my version of faith somehow contributed to my thinking I didn't have to listen in the first place?

As a child, I often wandered the hallways of our little Baptist church gazing at prominently displayed pictures of Jesus, the Lamb of God, meekly holding an innocent lamb in one hand and a simple wooden staff in the other hand; Jesus, the Light of the World, proclaiming Good News to all, a gregarious smile spread across his face; Jesus, the Son of God, sitting on a rock all by himself as he talked to the Father. In all of these paintings, his skin, without an imperfection or a blemish, shone porcelain and white, kind of like mine. And in most of the pictures, he sported a perfect California tan, our Messiah a brawny double for David Hasselhoff. A singular image was seared in my mind, making Jesus into an image of masculinity and gentleness, of hope and optimism, of confidence and whiteness.

This was my Jesus. This was the Jesus I desperately wanted the rest of the world to know. And I wasn't alone.

In the early 1940s, *Head of Christ* by American artist Warner Sallman became the standard image of Jesus for churches around the world. His depiction, complete with golden brown hair and suntanned skin, was reproduced more than half a billion times by the end of the twentieth century.[1] The painting didn't merely grow in popularity, it exploded, altogether changing the way Christians and non-Christians alike imagined the Christ.

Prior to this rendering, throughout the Middle Ages and the Renaissance, famed painters of European descent created their own versions of Jesus. In 1580, El Greco ("The Greek"), an architect, painter, and sculptor during the Spanish Renaissance, painted *Christ Carrying the Cross,* portraying Jesus with large doe eyes, elfish ears, and light porcelain skin.[2] His art was influenced by both his Greek Orthodox roots and the Catholic Counter-Reformation, and some critics question whether Jesus' skin color was merely a poor lighting mistake. Did the darkened, stormy scene behind the Son of God accidentally make his face appear lighter than intended, paler than El Greco believed God to look, or was the color of his skin intentional, a nod to beliefs of racial inferiority already present in the early church?

Rembrandt is also said to have changed the face of Jesus more than any other artist of his time. In *The Supper at Emmaus* (1601), Jesus eats with the two men he had just introduced his resurrected self to while on the road to Emmaus. The men in the painting gaze at him in astonishment, while a servant boy looks on from the back corner. Meanwhile, Jesus gazes heavenward in innocence, coifed and curled brown locks flowing down the front of his chest, an angelic halo beaming from his head. All four of the men look to be of European descent. Nearly four decades later, in *Head of Christ* (1648), Jesus looks decidedly Mediterranean, evident by the color of his skin and his facial features. As time went on, Rembrandt "shifted away from Jesus as the heroic superbeing of antiquity towards a more human, more accessible to believers, and, perhaps, truer face of Christ," writes *Big Think* columnist Bob Duggan.[3] The color of

Jesus' skin is only slightly changed at best, but it leads some historians to wonder whether the artist used a Jewish model for inspiration, given the Netherlands' fascination with biblical history in the seventeenth century.

But where did these images of a white Jesus originate? What led these painters of European descent, whose artistic renderings the American public adopted as their own, to depict Jesus as white in the first place? In 2001, the makers of BBC One's *Son of God* series sought to answer why Jesus is often depicted as white, calling out an assumed image of Jesus as having "light-brown, shoulder-length hair. A slim, bearded and, above all, white face."[4] The New Testament gives no physical description of Jesus, so it's clear that the images fixed in my mind came from paintings hung on church walls, Precious Moments illustrations in storybook Bibles, and reruns of *The Ten Commandments* starring Charlton Heston. (Heston, of course, played Moses in the movie, but as a child, Moses and Jesus were one and the same in my mind. Call it what you may, I liken it to a creative interpretation of the transfiguration.)

In an effort to answer the question, though, the makers of the series looked both at the symbolism and at the culture surrounding whiteness. The color white is often seen as a symbol of purity or innocence, with various depictions of a fluffy white lamb[5] made real for the blamelessness of Christ. And culturally, just as many of the paintings now regarded as famous were rendered by artists in Western Europe, many Western Europeans wanted to believe their God was fair-skinned—not because they desired an image made in their likeness but because of the "cultural baggage of the Crusades, in which non-whites were seen as non-believers."[6] By deeming themselves superior to those with dark skin, white people passed down images of a lily-white Christ, images of a Jesus who looked more like them than like a Mediterranean man weathered by the elements of the sun and sea. It's no wonder an image of whiteness lived in my mind, both of what God must have looked like and also of what God's followers were supposed to look like.

Of course, I also don't have to delve too deeply into conversations of race to realize that race is a social construct, an idea for which no coherent, fixed definition exists.[7] Race is a manmade invention, an idea thought up by those of European descent, by those who felt the need to separate and classify based on outward appearances alone. It's like a piece of paper out of which two circles are cut: a big circle and a small circle, a circle of domination and a circle of inferiority. Out of these circles, society can see who's in and who's out, clearly defined categorizations a guide for the way we perceive and treat others. In that way, race is not in any sense of the word biological. "There is no gene or cluster of genes common to all blacks or all whites," writes Angela Onwuachi-Willig in an article for *The New York Times*. "Were race 'real' in the genetic sense, racial classifications for individuals would remain constant across boundaries."[8]

In the mid-1600s, Francois Bernier, a French traveling physician, was the first to sort the peoples of the world into four categories of color: white, yellow, brown, and black.[9] Five years later, another Frenchman, Jean-Baptiste-Simeon Chardin, added to Bernier's thoughts when he, upon "traveling through the Middle East in search of precious stones, put forth his ideas about the beautiful, naked, light-skinned women he saw in the Caucasus Mountains, a region bordered by what are now Chechnya and Georgia."[10] Not withstanding the effect of the Crusades on Western Europe, within a century, pale skin became the beauty standard for whites, and affected artistic depictions of the Christ. In her book *Waking Up White*, Debby Irving cites additional factors such as the white European colonization of Asia, Africa, and the Americas, and the role and mission of white

Christian missionaries, who believed a "white, Christian way was the superior way and that 'taming the heathens' in order to save their souls required a full-on conversion to Christianity."[11] By the time early settlers reached the Americas, categorizations of dominance, based on social theory and backed by religious beliefs, were already deeply rooted.

In 1619, British colonies brought the first African slaves to the banks of Jamestown, Virginia, sewing the atrocities of racism and white supremacy onto the fabric of our country. Although they were classified as indentured servants, in the article "The Evolution: Slavery to Mass Incarceration," public-interest lobbyist Aristotle Jones reminds readers about the reality of plantation life, a reality so far from the wonders of my suburban upbringing. Just as the market for tobacco and cotton spiked, the demand for land and for labor to work the land increased. As a result, those who were classified as servants became classified as slaves, thus losing their rights entirely. Meanwhile, slave owners retained complete power over black and brown men, women, and children, who became legally recognized property instead of humans who could work for a fixed amount of time. "During these years of terrorism, millions of slaves in America were traumatized, humiliated, beaten, devastated and killed. Husbands and wives, parents and children could not protect themselves from being sold away from one another."[12] I think about what it would be like to be torn from the ones I love most, to feel my children's flesh ripped from my embrace, to stretch my arms in want of my father. But then I stop, because I remember that it's only a dream and there's only so far my imagination can take me. Mine is the choice of haunted make-believe, but those who were enslaved lived the horror everyday.

I also don't have to think too far back to remember the lessons taught me by Mr. Freeman in the seventh grade and Mr. Johnson in the eleventh grade, and by various professors in college and in seminary. Just as bells signaled the end of classes, so they signaled the end of conversations. I didn't have to connect the dots to an oppression that started when humans that the state considered to be chattel stepped onto Virginia's shore, when disenchanted systems favored those whose skin looked more like mine than like the man I loved. I didn't understand that although the framers of the constitution called for freedom, their plantation owners called for slavery. I didn't see these clear discrepancies, inconsistencies that let me step in and out of conversations as I pleased.

And a narrative of slavery continues, today's shackles the injustice of mass incarceration of black and brown men, and systems of whiteness that do not affirm equality, liberty, and justice for all. It's hard to ignore the facts when "more African American adults are under correctional control today—in prison or jail, on probation or parole—than were enslaved in 1850, a decade before the Civil War began. The mass incarceration of people of color is a big part of the reason that a black child born today is less likely to be raised by both parents than a black child born during slavery."[13] Likewise, it's impossible for me not to see the threads of injustice woven throughout the fabric of our country, when, "on the domestic front in 2015, 40 percent of unarmed people killed by police were black men, yet black men make up only 6 percent of the national population."[14] I may be a fellow sojourner rather than a scholar, but one truth remains: although race is a social construct, the effects *of* race are real and material. I don't have to squint my eyes too hard to see its destructiveness on those who were once labeled three-fifths of a human because of the black and brown color of their skin, just as I don't have to look that far to see how beliefs about whiteness burrowed into every nook and cranny of the church, even into images that make Christ look more like me than his dark-skinned, Middle Eastern self.

*M*onths after my conversation with Keisa, James and I sat across from each other at our dining room table, as we'd done a hundred times before. Our hands stretched across the worn wood, over divots and scratches and indentations, signs of the weathering I never imagined I would experience in marriage. For me, realizations of hurt and pain always come later, hours, days, years after a conversation, when words buried in my soul finally burrow out into the light.

"I'm complicit, aren't I?" I asked James, ashamed as snapshots of the past flooded my mind. I thought about how quick I was to brag about the kids of color I worked with, about how although San Mateo County boasted a 61 percent white majority,[15] I spent most of my time working with teenagers who didn't look a whole lot like me. "They need an adult to mentor and befriend them," I'd say. "And for some reason, they seem to want to hang out with weird, quirky grown-up me." This was my image of the work I got to do, these broken teenagers like baby chicks waddling behind their proud mama hen. To be honest, though, I liked hanging out with them because I liked the way we looked together. I liked hanging out with them because they made me feel like I was helping to fight racism, our coffee dates tearing down walls of injustice, one sip at a time. But I also liked hanging out with them because they seemed to be the ones who most needed fixing, the ones who could most benefit from friendship with an adult like me.

My hand still clasped in his, I bowed my head, tears welling in my eyes.

"Maybe we're all complicit," he finally said.

"Honey, you of all people are not complicit in this conversation," I replied, nevertheless grateful for his empathy.

Not unlike the Christian missionaries who first descended on American soil, not only had I bought into images of a white Jesus but

I had also purchased in bulk images of the white savior within me. I always had good intentions, embracing the mentality of a hero as I took up the white man's burden.[16] But somehow I had gotten it into my head that those who most needed my help probably didn't look like me, believing it my duty to seek and to save those whose skin happened to be darker than mine.

As I sat in our dining room that evening, I knew the fault was mine. And just as I wondered whether this paradox of beauty and struggle would always be, I wondered whether a thousand utterances of repentance would ever be enough to say I'm sorry, to take away the pain I had caused. Should I quit? Had my time in ministry begun to come to a close?

But before I could think too much about next steps, something changed it all.

CHAPTER 10

Little Caramels

We found out the day I walked into the church sanctuary feeling woozy, like someone had decided to play beach volleyball in my stomach.

"Wow, you feeling okay there, tiger?" my friend David asked me.

I gulped back queasy burps. "Yeah, I'm not really sure what's going on," I replied.

James and I had hosted a small going-away party with some of our neighbors the night before, gathering to say goodbye to Laurie and Mel with carryout pizza, an impromptu dance party, and a viewing of *Bridesmaids* on the big screen television. I hadn't had too much to eat or drink, that much I knew, but by the end of the church service, I wanted nothing more than to cozy up on the couch under a blanket and take a nap, maybe for the rest of the afternoon, maybe for the next week.

"Is it flu season already?" I asked James a couple of hours later when I hadn't moved an inch.

"Well, whatever it is, I'm not catching it!" he replied, spraying Lysol into the air so heavily I had to cough back the fumes.

Exhaustion had overcome every limb of my body, but if it wasn't the flu, did I have mono? Had the burdens of ministry wreaked havoc on my weary soul? Then it hit me: shaking my head deliriously, I stood up and walked to the bathroom. A couple of minutes later, a maniacal kind of laughter confirmed my suspicion and woke the napping husband who hadn't wanted to catch his wife's sickness: I was pregnant.

*O*ver the next nine months, my body was not my own. An alien had taken up residence in my uterus, growing from the size of a seed to a raisin to a grape, from a kumquat to a lemon to a grapefruit. James and I hadn't known whether I would be able to get pregnant and have a baby—after all, we'd stood alongside several of our friends in their struggles with infertility. "We'll try," we had said, but we would remain open to what might not be in the cards for us.

But then, it was in the cards.

Exhaustion reared its ugly head at three o'clock every afternoon. Too tired to close my eyes, I watched *Law & Order: SVU* like it was my job. Maybe I could set my sights on a career involving the most heinous of crimes; surely watching eight seasons in two months' time qualified me to become part of New York City's elite squad of detectives. Six hours later, a carnivorous hunger consumed me: I'd stand in front of the refrigerator with the door wide open, tearing off chunks of rotisserie chicken, barefoot and pregnant in the kitchen.

I gained nearly forty pounds, even as I waddled once, twice, three times around the neighborhood every day with Mr. Darcy. I propped my feet up on the ottoman at night. I parked in the Expectant Parking area of Babies R Us when I shopped there, bewildered by the sheer number of options available to new parents. I avoided tomatoes, because the savory fruit gave me heartburn, and I lamented the salsa and pizza I couldn't consume. I began calling our unborn son Little Caramel, desiring to keep the name we'd chosen a secret, not yet realizing that likening my future child's skin tone to the color of a piece of candy wasn't helping conversations about racial equality. That would come later.

But I also hadn't fully learned how to listen to my body when, halfway through my pregnancy, James and I found ourselves at Disney World for a work conference.

"I'll show Mickey and Minnie who's boss!" I shouted as we wound through the Magic Kingdom and Epcot Center with our friends. While the rest of the group rode rides, I rested on park benches or on sidewalks, waiting for their return.

"Are you sure you're okay?" James asked after a couple of hours as my gait got slower and my legs struggled to keep pace.

"I'm fine, I'm fine. You go on ahead," I said, shooing him back toward the rides. He'd never been to a Disney theme park before, and I wasn't about to let my pregnant body ruin the experience for him. But martyrdom did not befit me as I walked through the park in darkness on my way back to our hotel.

"This is not the happiest place on earth," I muttered, tears rolling down my face. It wasn't anyone's fault but my own. I still thought I could do all and be all, but the tiny human growing inside my body rejected any notion of my being Superwoman. Meanwhile, I carried what felt like the dead weights of Goofy and Pluto on my back, the ghosts of a thousand chipper cartoon characters mocking my every step.

"Do you want a piggyback ride?" my friend Guy asked. He had left the group with me out of his own tiredness and to check on his wife, who had stayed behind at the hotel that day. But he wasn't about to mistake my tears for sadness: those were tears of exhaustion and weariness, tears of a woman who shouldn't have been walking so many thousands of steps in the first place.

I shook my head. No self-respecting woman would let a man half her size carry her on his back through Main Street, USA. Slinging my arm around his shoulder, he slowed his gait, his body carrying the weight of my tired bones as we crept slowly toward the bus.

Within an hour, I was snuggled under a pile of blankets in our hotel room, empty cheeseburger wrapper and chocolate milkshake cup on the table beside me. When James returned, apologies filled the air.

"I shouldn't have left you by yourself," he said. "I should have gone with you. We should have come back here together."

"Yeah, maybe. But it was Disney World! I probably should have just stayed at the hotel and lounged by the pool all afternoon."

"Well, I'm sorry."

"And I'm sorry too." I realized there was only so much I could do, as a human and as a human who carried a tinier human inside of her. It was time to hang up the Superwoman cape.

Nearly six months later, I worked until two days shy of my due date, determined to reserve as much time off to spend with our son after his birth. But when I hit forty-one weeks and a pedicure didn't work to bring on the birth, and forty-two weeks and acupuncture didn't do the trick either, my doctor scheduled an induction.

James hung neatly typed birthing instructions on the hospital room wall: "You will not administer Cara pain medicine of any kind. You will not administer an epidural, even if she asks for it. You will not give the baby formula after the birth." I bounced on the yoga ball in the corner of the hospital room, the soothing sounds of the HypnoBirthing soundtrack echoing the rhythms of my body. Tubes poked out of my wrists and out of the tops of my hands; multiple IV lines fed saline into me because my levels were dangerously low. Finally, thirty-six hours after our arrival, my water broke. I clutched the side of the hospital bed, unable to get out unassisted, unable to walk around the room and grunt and moan with the contractions as I craved.

"Hold my hand, please!" I whispered to the night nurse when she came to check on me at four in the morning.

"Wake up your husband, lady," she whispered back. Sleeping soundly in a corner cot lay James, earplugs blocking his ability to hear my groans. "Yo, husband!" she yelled across to him. "It's time!" James sat up, bounded across the room, and took my hand into his own. As the hours passed, he fed me ice chips, closing his eyes with every contraction, pressing his chest against my back, trying to absorb the pain. And twelve hours later, after an emergency C-section, James peered over the side of the curtain, watching the doctors unwrap the umbilical cord from our baby's neck.

"It's a boy!" he whispered, his eyes filling with tears. And placing his son on my chest, we two became three.

*W*e named him Canon, a nod to a student I met as a camp speaker the summer before. The word canon merely means the order of things, be it music or laws or even the books of the Bible. "Canon, Canon, Canon," we'd say, whispering his name in the middle of the night and at the height of the afternoon. He was our little campfire, a blazing light we couldn't stare at or coo over enough, an angel baby who ate when he was supposed to eat and slept when he was supposed to sleep.

Eight weeks after his birth, it was time for me to return to work. I took Canon with me everywhere I went, both as primary caregiver and as nonprofit outreach director. I could set my own schedule, working from home in the mornings and taking him along with me to donor meetings and tutoring sessions in the afternoons. I could breastfeed him in secluded rooms of the church building where I had an office, and I could position a blanket for him to play on, squeaky toys and squishy stuffed giraffes his kingdom come.

Not all went according to plan, though. Thousands of dollars of deficit loomed over the ministry I oversaw. I wondered if I would ever see another paycheck, if I could ever raise the money to see our programs thrive. But part of the financial hardship stemmed from a loss of key donors while I was on maternity leave. I couldn't understand what had gone wrong in such a short time until the rumors finally made their way to me, lies about me and about my choices in leadership. By the time the truth was revealed—truth that cleared my integrity but made me feel like a failure nonetheless—it was too late. I was undone by exhaustion.

I couldn't do it anymore. I couldn't do it all and I couldn't be it all, not for my son and not for those I cared for in ministry.

"Cara, what do you think happened?" my boss asked me when I gave notice less than two months after I'd returned to work. I shrugged as tears streamed down my face. A hundred different explanations ran through my mind, each of which seemed good enough and not good enough all at the same time, but each true nonetheless.

"Just get me out," I finally whispered. It was time, albeit sooner and messier than I'd ever anticipated. I didn't know what would happen next, but I knew it would be better and slower and quieter, with Canon by my side. And I held dreams of becoming a writer and a speaker someday, though how that would happen, I had no clue. I just knew I had to get out of my job in ministry, that *this* was not the place for me anymore. My time was up, even if I felt lost in the prospect of the unknown, even if it felt like the future was a liminal space.

By the time Canon turned a year old, I felt like I was finally gaining my sea legs as a stay-at-home mom. Our days were quiet: he ate, he played, he slept. We went to parks and we took long walks;

we bulldozed our way through stacks of picture books, and when he napped, I wrote for an hour or two, the words buried within me a lifeline to the outside world and a healing that happens only when pen meets paper. Our life was quieter, our world smaller, but we discovered a new gentleness, a tenderness that seemed to fit our family of three just perfectly.

*W*hat's another kid?" James and I asked one another, laughing at the question. It had been nearly a year since I'd left ministry, and with Canon nearing the eighteen-month mark, we figured it was as good a time as any to try to have another child. But just as before, it took me a couple of months to realize I might be pregnant, to finally run to the bathroom for a pregnancy stick.

I didn't get it when I bought a jumbo-sized box of frozen cheeseburgers and returned them to Costco a couple of days later, declaring to the woman behind the counter, "These cheeseburgers are bad! They gave me food poisoning!" Never in my life had a cheeseburger made me throw up, I wanted to add.

And I didn't get it when I went on a writing weekend with a couple of girlfriends soon after the cheeseburger incident. "I wonder if I stayed in the hot tub too long last night. It's like I'm pregnant or something," I said to my friend Erin after vomiting in a coffee-shop bathroom and returning to my bed with a vicious headache. All I could do was lie there and watch the first season of *Scandal,* my dreams of saving the world through my words supposedly derailed by an overheated Jacuzzi.

And I didn't get it when we hosted a couple of families on Christmas Eve and the eggnog made me gag and my eyes watered at the smell of cracked crab. "Does anyone else smell that? Can you smell that? Good Lord, I hope we didn't buy bad seafood!" I exclaimed.

But a couple of days later, after my pants didn't seem to fit and I couldn't climb up a hilly San Franciscan street without losing my breath, two positive blue lines confirmed the truth others had begun to suspect: I was pregnant.

Nearly nine months later, James and I drove to the hospital for a scheduled C-section, the doctor having declared my body good at growing babies but not so good at birthing them. Just as he'd done before, James joined me in the operating room, raising his child into the air seconds after he emerged.

"It's a boy!" my husband announced, his tears no less apparent than the first time he'd spoken the words. This son we named Theodore, his name meaning "one who is loved by God." Canon's placid demeanor was never his brother's, who instead had a boisterous, zero to sixty in three point nine seconds or less type of personality. He ate around the clock, his schedule as unpredictable as the earthquakes that sometimes shook the ground where we lived, his very essence the kind that would move mountains someday.

*S*oon enough, it was time to send Canon to preschool, and to fill out a massive stack of paperwork: mother's name, father's name, sibling's name, address, phone number, doctor's information, immunization records, likes, dislikes. The questions seemed unending. My pen glided over the first page, but when I got to the second page, I stopped: the words "circle one only," an instruction to pick a single ethnic origin for my mixed-race son.[1]

I shook my head, pen wavering between "black" and "white," between two equal parts of the whole. My mind raced back to the standardized tests I took in Mrs. Windemere's third-grade class, in Mrs. Poehler's seventh-grade English class, in Mr. Austen's tenth-grade biology class. Had I ever wavered when it came to bubbling in the one that applied to me, the one labeled "white"? I had never hesitated because there was only one bubble I *could* fill in, only one made for the color of my skin.

It also never occurred to me to ask why, to question why the US government asks for "the nations of origin for Asian and Latino people, tribal affiliation for American Indian people, and include 'African American' (a specific ethnic group within the racial category 'black'), but does not ask 'white' people to identify their ethnicity or nation of origin."[2] But with demographics changing so rapidly because of broader cultural acceptance of interracial couples and multicultural families in the United States, multiracial births now make up 7 percent of all births.[3] Although racial categories of mulatto, octoroon, and quadroon (all denoting varying degrees of blackness) existed on the 1890 US Census, officials removed them ten years later, judging "the data 'of little value and misleading.'"[4] A little more than half a century later, the 1960 census instructed those who were mixed race to identify with their minority race. It wasn't until 2000, when large majorities of Hispanics could not identify with standard categories of race, that the census allowed respondents to bubble in more than one category, self-identifying race and ethnicity to their liking.[5]

In that moment, holy resistance found its way in, wriggling onto the paper of the archaic application. I felt the scope of my pen widen, creating an oblong circle around the words "black" and "white." Anger rose within me, the steam of injustice creeping up from stomach to chest to throat. I prayed my minor act of rebellion would be a movement against ignorance, against racism, against entire systems that didn't see anything wrong with asking parents and caregivers to "circle one only." I thought of the God who believes in me, the one I call Creator, Father, and sometimes, when I'm feeling particularly dangerous, Divine Mother too.

I thought about how God must have laid on a fluffy bed of clouds, twiddling elephant-sized thumbs and dreaming up the perfect combination of Canon and Theo, and you and me, and every other human on the face of the earth. I thought of his son, Word Made Flesh, who taught his friends and enemies alike to love unconditionally, to cherish the particularities, and to circle in all of the boxes without apology, the advantage ours for the taking.

But I also thought about how God delights not in uniformity but in diversity, not in homogeneity but in the differences that make us *us,* in the same beauty of dissimilarity that causes us to circle multiple bubbles in the first place. It made me think about one interpretation I read about the Tower of Babel, "when God divided the world into ethnic-language enclaves. God's love for diversity is clearly stated in Paul's message for the philosophers at the Areopagus: 'From one ancestor he made all nations to inhabit the whole earth, and he allotted the times of their existence and the boundaries of the places where they would live, so that they would search for God and perhaps grope for him and find him—though indeed he is not far from each one of us.'"[6] For this master of sky and land was also the creature maker, the one who created the entire human race just so we could find him, so in our blackness and our whiteness and in every color in between, we could say, "Hey, look! We're the God-created."

I stuffed Canon's application into an envelope and sealed it, deed done, whispers of the Holy Spirit heeded. Shame would not take up room in our house, not on a preschool application and not when it came to the diverse beauty of my family. But first, I had to start giving my children credit for who they already were and for what they already knew.

CHAPTER 11

Imago Dei

I sat poolside on a hotel rooftop in Birmingham, Alabama. My feet dangled in the water as the boys swam in the kiddie pool with their older cousin James, hot southern sun beating down on us all. The heat was just right—not too hot, not too muggy. *I could live here. I could do this,* I thought. The kids shrieked and yelled as they raced from one end of the pool to the other, joy their constant companion, an undeniable bond of kinship theirs alone.

With one eye on the boys and one on my book, I stole glances toward the water after every paragraph, oblivious when my father-in-law walked over and sat down on the lounger to my right.

"So," he said to me, the word a sentence in and of itself. Whenever James and I flew from the West Coast to the South once or twice a year, we steadied ourselves for The Talk, when the great patriarch sat down to chat with each of us separately. It was here that a bearded old man dressed in khaki pants, long-sleeve white-collared shirt, black velcro tennis shoes, and a straw hat sat next to a middle-aged woman clad solely in a black bandeau swimsuit from Target.

"So, how are you?" I replied, ready for his words.

"You need to give them more credit," he said, pointing toward the water. He paused in thought. This is how Granddaddy speaks:

although he knows what he wants to say, his words do not come quickly. He is southern to the bone, slow like a spoonful of molasses. He chews each thought; he kneads each point. And each pause feels like an eternity to me. "They know. They already know. They get it. They see color." His fingers jabbed the air with each point, begging me to understand. "And you have to give them credit for what they already know, for *who* they already are."

I ripped out a page from the back of my paperback book. "May I borrow a pen, sir?" I pointed to the handful of pens tucked into the pocket protector of his shirt. Whatever he had to say, I needed not to forget it anytime soon.

"You dealt with the issue, which was you. No one understands the depths of the race issue because they haven't lived it; they haven't experienced it like you have."

"But I—"

He held up his hand to stop me. It was not my place to disagree or interject. My job was to listen.

"Lincoln and Obama hold one thing in common: they were voted into office for unresolved issues of race. And these issues are gonna remain." He paused. "But your study of religion, the training you have received, plays a bigger part in this discussion. So stop worrying about too many things! Stop trying to solve the things that are out of your control. But do understand how much they already know. And do understand how much you already know too." He pointed again to the boys and then to me, my pen scribbling furiously on the worn piece of paper. Would I ever believe the words he spoke over me?

"Nobody! Nowhere! Anytime! Can solve the problems of anybody else. All they can do is understand."

I nodded, hand cramped from intensely writing down his thoughts. I knew my father-in-law had read a number of the articles

I had written, essays about my journey toward racial justice, stories about learning how to honor Canon and Theo's biracial identities. But he saw through it all. He knew I didn't yet believe in the power of love already written in my life, in the power of love's fire already present in the lives of my young sons. He knew I still had a lot of believing left to do.

*G*randdaddy's words left me with more questions than answers. I knew that leaning into the story already written on my life could come only with time, but I could dig into Christian tradition through my own theological training. Maybe someday I would study more about Islamic, Jewish, and Hindu interpretations of justice and unpack similarities of wholeness in Buddhism. But for now, I would look into what the Bible had to say about racial justice. I would read more about how Jesus responded to race, if he even responded at all.

In Genesis 1:26–28, the author lays out an account of creation: "Then God said, 'Let us make human beings in our image, to be like us. They will reign over the fish in the sea, the birds in the sky, the livestock, all the wild animals on the earth, and the small animals that scurry along the ground. So God created human beings in his own image. In the image of God he created them; male and female he created them. Then God blessed them and said, 'Be fruitful and multiply. Fill the earth and govern it. Reign over the fish in the sea, the birds in the sky, and all the animals that scurry along the ground'" (NLT).

As a student, I'd heard the text more times than I could remember, but these holy words authored by Moses tended to go in one ear and out the other. Like the adherents of many other religions, Christians believe that God was intimately involved in the most intricate aspects of creation, from the creation of water and sky and land, to slithery snakes and feathery birds, to humankind too. Some people view this account literally, while others look at it metaphorically, but regardless of how I looked at it, I still questioned how race fit into that order. If the conversation started here, with humans designed for relationship with God, then the verses weren't merely about the one who dreamed it all up and created women and men as colaborers in the work. They were about human beings, about how each and every person on this earth bears the divine stamp, the *imago Dei*. Every person, no matter the color of their skin, no matter their race or ethnicity or culture, no matter their religion or sexuality, no matter the other fill-in-the-blank excuses we use to categorize each other, bears an innate resemblance to the Creator. Every life matters simply because it is God's.

Soon after that trip to the South, James and I had a conversation with Canon.

"Who's that?" Canon asked when the four of us were riding together in the car. I looked out the window to where he was pointing, his finger pressed against the car window, inches, it seemed, from a homeless woman sitting on the corner. Her hair was dirty and matted, a worn "Help, Pleas. god bless" sign perched on her lap.

"Well, buddy, that's a person," I replied. Canon paused before pointing another fifty feet up the road to a young man with spiky pink hair riding a skateboard down the sidewalk.

"Who's that?"

"Well, that's a person too." And then he asked the question every small child is prone to ask.

"Why?"

"Because persons are humans, buddy."

"Why?"

"Well, because humans matter. You and me, we matter, even if we look different from one another. Every single person on this earth is a human, and every single one of them matters just because they're a human." I glanced across the console to James, a thousand questions filling the space between us: *Do you think he understands? Do you think he gets the* imago Dei *stamped on each of us, that even in our differences a deeper, greater truth exists, that we are God's and God is ours, and that's all that counts?* A lopsided grin spread across James' face and he shook his head: never had my theological education trained me for conversations with a three-year-old, nor had life prepared either one of us for the conversations that come with parenthood. Canon, meanwhile, just stared out the window, looking for more persons, I guess.

But those three verses in Genesis also end with a command for humans to fill the earth. In *Roadmap to Reconciliation,* Dr. Brenda Salter McNeil writes of "the cultural mandate," the part of the creation account that "reveals God's desire for the earth to be filled with a great diversity of races and peoples."[1] Just as God commanded his people to be fruitful and multiply, he commanded them to fill the earth and govern it—the result of this great and holy migration a heaping platter of difference: "Different stories. Different words. Different myths, songs, styles of communication, food, clothing."[2] God imprinted humanity with the style of the divine, with cultural difference and diversity in mind.

I thought about the homeless woman perched on the corner and about the boy with spiky pink hair who rode his skateboard down the street. I thought about Canon and Theodore, about the two little boys who had stolen my heart, whose slobbery kisses and tackle-knee hugs made me swoon. I thought about James, about how I knew he was The One when I couldn't picture my life without him. I thought about Gaga and Papa, and Nana and Granddaddy, about the unlikely intersection of our family trees, their tangled roots sometimes crazy enough to make you shake your head in wonder. I thought about my best friend, Mindy, and her basketball-loving son, and I thought about Keisa and all the kids I used to work with in ministry. As each picture flashed across my mind, I saw light skin and dark skin, curly hair and straight hair, smiles and frowns, laughter and tears. And through our common humanity, I saw the color of life.

But although every human has been made in the image of God, because of the systems in place in our country today, the power of dominion has not been reserved for everyone.[3] I would give my children the world if I could, an entire universe of water and land and rivers and trees theirs for the taking. I would buy my husband a valiant white stallion for the miles his legs have walked, the thunder of galloping hooves the applause for every day he's risen up against systems that didn't intend for him to thrive. This I would do, for though I come as one, I stand as ten thousand.[4] And until the tens of thousands who stand beside me taste the power of dominion so rightfully given them as image-bearers too, I am not free.

For as American Jewish poet Emma Lazarus once wrote, "Until we are all free, we are none of us free. Today, wherever we are free, we are at home."[5]

*A*s I think about this glorious stamping, my mind wanders past the Father to the Son, to the name often used as an excuse to devalue or ignore the *imago Dei* in other human beings. In an effort to get right the tenets of the faith, it's like we forgot to look at the source of faith itself, neglecting to notice how Jesus responded to the people around him.

In John 4, Jesus interacts with a Samaritan woman at a well. Not only had he gone out of his way to a town called Sychar, but he'd arrived in the middle of the day, without a bucket to drink from, at a time when he knew no else would be there. He knew he would meet her and her alone, that she wouldn't have been welcome with the other women early in the morning when they gossiped and laughed together. But Jesus always looks for the outsider. So he asks her for a drink, pushing through barriers of gender and ethnicity, because in those days a man did not ask a woman for a drink of water unless he also wanted her for sex. And Jews did not ask Samaritans for help, for they believed them to be ethnic half-breeds, worshipers of false gods.

The woman asks him questions, questions about religion and about the magical elixir of living water he's just mentioned, and he replies, "Everyone who drinks this water will be thirsty again, but whoever drinks the water I give them will never thirst. Indeed, the water I give them will become in them a spring of water welling up to eternal life."[6] When she begs for a drink of this water, he asks her to go get her husband, a reply conservative theologians point to as proof of her sin. *Look! She slept around. Look! She really, really needed Jesus because she was a sexually immoral woman.* They don't think about the other side of the story, that in second-century Judaism a woman had no rights in marriage: if a woman was barren, her husband could divorce her. If he didn't like the way she pounded the wheat and barley, he could discard her. If he believed she was ugly, he could throw her to the side.[7]

The reader doesn't know why she's been with a handful of men in her lifetime because that's not the point of the story. Instead, the point lies in the response of the one who calls himself the Living Water and in the way God treats everyone with dignity. Jesus comes to the woman with a need she is equipped to meet: she can draw water from the well. And in doing so, their exchange is mutual. He doesn't hold power over her, nor does she have to change or conform to his social perspective.

Instead, through their interaction, the woman no longer felt shame but empowerment. And because Jesus honored the particularities of her identity, including her ethnicity, her religion, and the stories of her past, she was changed—and couldn't help but introduce an entire community to him.

"If her particularities didn't matter, then why did John tell us all those details?" my friend Teylar asked over coffee one morning, further driving home the message I needed to hear. "He would have just said, 'Jesus met someone at the well.' But the particularities mattered deeply to Jesus, and so do ours." Teylar's words rang in my ears, just as images of my sons and my husband, family and friends, neighbors and strangers floated through my mind. The particularities *did* matter to Jesus, particularities made manifest on the inside and on the outside, particularities that celebrate the diversity of our differences.

How I longed to celebrate those particularities too.

I knew I couldn't solve anybody else's problems, but I could pay attention to the particularities. I could recognize and honor the *imago Dei* in those around me.

When I was pregnant with Canon, I decided to give a weekly pregnancy report on my blog: surely people wanted to hear everything I had to say about maternity clothes, food cravings, strangers' absurd comments, and interesting observations. Not wanting to give away his name too early, I nicknamed my future son Little Caramel, a nod to the delicious color of his skin. At the same time, I decided to call James the HBH (Hot Black Husband), because he was my hot husband. And he happened to be a black man.

"It just rolls off your tongue!" I said one night over dinner, laughing at my own joke, never thinking to ask him what he thought of my newly minted name for him.

At that time, many of the bloggers I followed created kitschy nicknames to call their loved ones, sometimes to protect them, other times to make a reader laugh. I vowed to do the same, but when it came to my nickname for James, I also wanted to punch Christian patriarchy in the face. Male pastors around the globe filled their pulpits with talk about their "smokin' hot wife" on Sunday mornings, about the "blonde babe" whose servant's heart (and svelte, sensual body) was second only to God's. If they could so blatantly objectify women, certainly I could fight against the powers that be and call them on their game. But I also thought the nicknames would help break down barriers of race and ethnicity with my readers and with the teenagers I worked with in ministry. Surely people would see that I wasn't just a white lady but a white lady in intimate relationship with a person of color who had an innate understanding of race.

But I did so at the expense of my husband and my son, their racial identities my gain.

And I didn't stop there. After I left ministry, I began writing in various spaces around the internet. The monikers became a part of my stories and a part of my bylines: "Cara Meredith is a writer and speaker. She loves dinners around the table and stacks of good books. She lives with the HBH (Hot Black Husband) and their Little Caramel in San Francisco, California." Once again, I believed the nicknames gave me credibility with readers of color and with those already involved in conversations of race and justice. When invitations for different podcasts came in, I used the monikers on the airwaves, still thinking I was somehow opening up dialogue.

But then, even as their nicknames rolled off my tongue, the real names of black and brown victims reached my ears. Trayvon Martin. Michael Brown. Eric Garner. Amadou Diallo. Jordan Davis. Rekia Boyd. Ezell Ford. John Crawford III. Tamir Rice. Yvette Smith. Freddie Gray. The Mother Emanuel Nine. Sandra Bland. Laquan McDonald. Jamar Clark. Botham Jean. Their names had been there all along, but I hadn't taken the time to listen and notice them in the first place. The more I heard their names, the more their names became a part of me; the more their names became a part of me, the more their names weren't merely names but real, fleshy lives lost in the fallout of racism and white supremacy.[8] Although I intended the nicknames of my husband and son purely for fun, by continuing to identify them by their appearance, I robbed them of their dignity. I missed the whole point in the fight for equality, because this wasn't a matter of being funny or breaking down walls anymore. This was a matter of life and death.

For we humans are knit by our humanity, by the *imago Dei* present in every single one of us. We are bound by a law of mutuality that connects us, by "the belief in a universal bond of sharing that connects all humanity,"[9] called *ubuntu*. Although the word originates from the Nguni Bantu people, Desmond Tutu made the phrase universal. For here, a person is a person through other people. Here, I am because you are. Here, a human-to-human kind of honoring happens only because of the humanity that binds us together, and here, we belong, one to the other.

When injustice affecting those in our own back yards and halfway across the country fills news headlines, we carry the injustice of others within us. As Dr. Martin Luther King Jr. wrote from a jail cell, "Injustice anywhere is a threat to justice everywhere. We are caught in an inescapable network of mutuality, tied in a single garment of destiny. Whatever affects one directly, affects all indirectly."[10] Through a single garment of destiny, I am tied to my black and brown brothers and sisters, and it's not about my relationship with a black man or about the bloodlines of mother to child, it's about the stamp of humanity present on you and on me.

Making a change then remains my only choice.

"If we are connected to each other, then our wellness—our flourishing—is also connected to others," writes Idelette McVicker, a child of South African apartheid.[11] Just as I desire wholeness for myself, I desire it for others, for this wholeness is not mine to keep. And so, nearly five years after I began using the monikers, I stopped.

James and I sat on opposite ends of our deep, brown leather couch, fanning our necks and faces in the broiling August heat. "A reader called my bluff," I said. "'How can you write and speak about issues of race and justice on the one hand, and call your husband the HBH and your children Little Caramels on the other hand? More important, how can you let others call them by these names, as if they are property?'" Her questions were the only burial ground I needed. I apologized to James, my words to him simultaneously a release of shame and a relief.

"Yeah, the names aren't helping the situation anymore," James replied, and that was all he had to say. My words had been a hindrance to him and to my brothers and sisters of color, start and end of story.

Later that evening, I made a public announcement on my website about the nickname I'd given James:

> Such a reference objectifies him. It devalues his identity by placing the "black" descriptor before his more important role as my husband. And in today's climate, where racial tension is the norm and white supremacy has been given permission to fly, we do not need *one more reason* to devalue black and brown lives.
>
> Calling him this name, wherever the space, is no longer helping the conversation.
>
> So, as of today, the HBH is retired. We've said our goodbyes. A new name will emerge for him, if necessary, in the future.

And if my name for him has offended you, I ask your forgiveness. I'm learning and I'm growing and I'm messing up on this journey, but more than anything, I desire that this be a safe space for all of us, and especially for my brothers and sisters of color. So, please, forgive me.[12]

I pushed "publish" and sent out the truth of my journey with some of its foibles and good intentions exposed for all to see. I knew it was right and I knew it had to happen.

But still, part of me wondered, would I ever understand problems of race? Would I ever actually get it?

CHAPTER 12

The Problem

*J*ames and I sat on the back porch of a small sea cottage listening to the water lapping underneath the deck at high tide. Four days away from it all, the four of us with my parents, couldn't have come at a better time. Both of us ached with exhaustion: he from the responsibilities of a high-pressure job, and I still feeling deeply inadequate to write a book about race and justice. I wondered whether I had any right to write a book on the subject at all.

I balanced a glass of iced tea in my hand as I sat transfixed by the glassy sea.

"You know," I said, "it has always been my privilege to step in and out of conversations of race. I can talk about it if I want to, when I want to, but if I don't want to, I can just turn the switch off. But I realize that's never been the case for you, nor is it the case for any person of color, nor will it be the case for our boys. And I realize it might not be the case for me anymore either." James nodded, the weight of the last week evident as his head fell heavily against the back of the weathered Adirondack chair.

Only four days before, the governor of Virginia had declared a state of emergency in Charlottesville: white supremacists from around the country had rallied against an elite group of clergy women and men gathered to resist racism. Delayed in the Jackson, Mississippi airport when it happened, I ached to return to the ones folded in my heart, to the same ones whose lives prompted vengeful lashings out of hate in the first place. As news headlines scrawled across the bottom of the screen, I watched the University of Virginia being torn apart by racial hatred nearly fifty-five years after my father-in-law's entrance into the University of Mississippi.

The vinyl chair in the airport gave no comfort as tears rolled down my cheeks. I didn't dare look around me: the last thing I wanted to see was indifference, a hundred eyes fixed to their cell phone screens instead of to the news. Would the hate ever end? Would black and brown lives ever be valued as citizens in their own country? The words of my father-in-law echoed in my mind: "Am I a citizen or am I not?" He'd asked this of the educational system, of his fellow Mississippians, of the president of the United States himself. And now, as history eerily repeated itself, I found myself asking the same question: "Are they citizens or are they not?"

If they are—if we are, as a whole—then no one is excused from the conversation. Instead of hate, we choose subversive joy and indefatigable faith. We hope for another way, for new paths forward, for healing truly to come to our land. We are hopeful for a resistance that accompanies the protesting cries of those who hope, for a true feast of those who resist.[1]

Back on the deck of the sea cottage, the air stood silent between us. The waves lapped beneath our feet. The occasional gull squawked overhead. Staring at a row of trees on the other side of the inlet, James grabbed my hand and held it tightly.

"Yes. It's an advantage to be able to turn the switch off," he finally said. It took a trip to Mississippi without him for me to realize this benefit, but I knew there was more to learn.

The week before, I'd left the boys in the care of their favorite babysitter and adopted older sister, Fernanda, and flew across the country to spend time with the Meredith side of the family. "Hold on. Correct me if I'm wrong," a friend had said to me days before I left. "But you're flying to the Deep South to visit your in-laws. And it's just you, no husband and no sons?" I nodded and laughed, wondering if she could detect the nervousness that grew like a ball of yeasty dough inside my belly. Visiting this side of the family without the one who had brought us together wasn't the norm, nor had I ever even thought about taking a trip like this. But I wanted to interview my father-in-law for the book, which I knew could happen only if I had him all to myself. Besides, if conversation waned, I figured I could get some writing in or visit significant historic sites around the state capital.

"So, you're a writer?" the large Dutch man on my left asked, peering at my laptop screen. I was on the second of two flights, heading to the Medgar Evers airport on a regional hopper plane.

"Yup." Just as I'd learned not to give my children more information than their questions warranted, I'd learned to do the same with big humans.

"And what do you write about?"

"Well, I write for online and print publications, mostly about faith-based issues, parenting, and," I paused, "issues of justice. But right now I'm working on my book." I pointed to the screen, a smile spread wide across my face. My eyes dared him to ask me another question.

"And what's your book about?"

"Oh, it's a memoir about my journey as a white woman toward issues of race."

"Well, all right, then, good luck with that!" Grabbing the airline magazine in the seat pocket in front of him, he sat mesmerized by Delta's quarterly flight information and the mechanical details of their jet-engine fleet.

The next morning, the scene wasn't all that different from previous visits. Judy, my mother-in-law, picked me up at a coffee shop not far from my hotel. She pulled me toward her when we met, slapping kisses on my cheeks, squeezing my body in a tight embrace. It had been too long. Lattes in hand, we drove back to their house on Meadowbrook Road, the familiarity of the gravel driveway, the simple one-story house, and overgrown vegetation all the welcome I craved. Late-summer rain swirled round us in a mist, humidity so thick you could almost taste the South on your tongue. "You know you're a true southerner when you stop whining about the weather," my father-in-law later said. Apparently, my northern roots shone through from the very beginning.

We hopped over mud puddles, aiming for islands of grass and dirt, hopeful we wouldn't land in the thirsty Mississippi mud. The news blared from inside the house, its presence a constant whenever the pair finished their daily chores.

"We're home!" she shouted, opening the front door. He was just as I suspected he would be: lounged in a recliner, transfixed by the stories on the plasma screen before him.

"Why, hello!" he bellowed, leaning back in his chair in an effort to hoist himself forward. He shook my hand, pulling me toward him.

"You know, he doesn't do that for everyone," Judy said.

"What? Hug them?" I asked.

She nodded. James Meredith didn't answer to anyone but himself. This she knew better than anyone, and this I would remember throughout the weekend and over the course of time as his daughter-in-law and as a devourer of forgotten history. I thought about a paragraph I'd read on the airplane less than twenty-four hours earlier: "James Howard Meredith was a character so colorful and complex, he could have sprung only from the rich soil of Mississippi. He seemed to dwell inside a myth of his own design, a realm often remote and impenetrable to other people. He was an obscure loner who before his thirtieth birth would engineer a stunning historical coup by mobilizing thousands of people to do his will, including the president and the Supreme Court of the United States. He was a supremely logical man whose reasoning would be misunderstood by practically everyone, a brilliant strategist who would be dismissed by many as being crazy."[2] But this colorful character also happened to be a normal older man, the father of my husband and the grandfather of my sons. More than any role or title, degree, or accolade bestowed upon him, he was family.

"I thought you and James could run a few errands together," Judy said after a couple of minutes. Lowering her voice, she added, "And please, whatever you do, don't let the man drive."

My father-in-law had had cataract surgery just the day before. Oversized black sunglasses shielded his eyes from the television screen and from us, from everything his eyes were still too sensitive to see. Doctors had warned him to take it easy for a week at least: no gym, no reading, and certainly no driving. We walked through darkened rooms of the house, passing splashes of neon and kitschy childhood memorabilia in one of my niece's rooms, and an old typewriter, a handful of framed photographs, a stack of library books, and a hoarder's paradise of loose, unfixed papers in his office. Did brilliance always look so messy?

"Give those to me!" he ordered, reaching for the keys in my hand as we stepped outside.

"Uh, Judy said I have to drive. You just had surgery."

"Judy's not the boss of me!"

"Yeah, but can you see?"

"I can see just fine! I been seeing my whole life!" He climbed into the driver's seat as I fastened the seat belt tightly around me. *Please, God, don't let this be the end—not for him, not for me. Give him the eyes to see. Literally. Please. Amen.* Pushing his cataract glasses up the bridge of his nose, he adjusted the bright red Ole Miss ball cap on his head and backed out of the driveway.

*M*aybe the key to expectations is not to have any expectations in the first place. I thought we could visit historic sites memorable to the movement. He thought we could visit the bank, the gym, the library, and the Chick-fil-A drive-thru. I thought we might finally bridge the communication gap between us, the bond we shared only heightened by our time together. Hard of hearing, he could barely hear a word I said, blaming it on my northern, younger, culturally inept ways. I'd throw my hands in the air: I just can't win. I can't wrestle keys from his hands and I can't heal the gaping differences between us.

But our differences didn't mean he didn't love my boys or me, so as it turned out, there wasn't a better way to start our time together. After all, I was the one who had entered his world. I was the one eager to understand the legacy of a man who'd helped to change our view of our country and the people in it. And that's when it hit me: love isn't always spoken by gushy crimson hearts or sentimental words. Sometimes love means opening your schedule to spend time with the mother of your grandsons. Sometimes love means showing off your world and letting someone taste the place that makes you *you.* And sometimes love means speaking the only truth you know, the last truths alive in your bones.

Shoulders hunched over the steering wheel, my father-in-law was as stubborn as ever despite the warm summer wind and rain and his cataract surgery. He drove into the parking lot of a bank, parking a full five feet from the curb. I trailed behind him as he made his deposit, garnering curiosity from every teller and patron within range. Their eyes seemed to say what their mouths wouldn't dare speak. *How do those two go together?* He led me into the manager's private office.

"Mr. Meredith, why it's great to see you!" A wide smile spread across her face. He was known in these parts.

"I have three grandsons, and this woman is the mother of two of them." I smiled in anticipation of her response. Had she expected a formal introduction or even a polite reciprocation of her greeting? Regardless of what she'd thought might happen, he had gotten right to the point, to the point of how we two fit together, for he was not one to waste his words. I shook her hand. You couldn't deny the man's pride for his family.

"You want me to drive now?" I asked, ready to get into the passenger seat in case he declined my offer. His eyebrows wriggled up his forehead like caterpillars creeping over the top of his thick black cataract frames. Without a word, he opened the driver's side door and climbed in.

A couple of minutes later, the scene repeated itself when we got to the gym.

"Mr. Meredith, it's so great to see you!"

"Mr. Meredith, didn't you just have surgery yesterday? What are you doing out of your house?" An indomitable, defiant force within him laughed aloud at their questions. *You think eye surgery's gonna get James Meredith down?*

We made our way to his table, to the place he sits every morning after getting in his miles on the treadmill. And to every person who passed us, he said the same words: "Did you know [pause] that I have three grandsons, and this woman right here is the mother of the two youngest ones?" He didn't call me by name, nor did he mention the one with whom I share a bed. But always he connected me to the next generation, to the two young boys who carry his crusade in their blood.

"Would you like to answer some questions my readers have for you?" I asked him, waiting for permission to proceed. "Here's the first one: 'What can I as a white woman do to help with racial reconciliation and justice?'" I glanced across the table at him, pen poised, ready to record in shorthand a lengthy dose of wisdom.

"Keep livin'," he finally mumbled, flicking his hand in the air. Wrong question.

"Okay, 'What public moment are you most proud of?'"

"You know, I went to Ole Miss and I never saw a thing. Not one teacher, not one student, not one marshal. And you know why? Because all of them, they take energy. And I don't waste my energy."

"So, integrating into the University of Mississippi was the proudest moment of your life?"

"That's not what I said! You're not listening! Now ask me something worthwhile, won't you?"

I folded the piece of paper in half and tucked it into the back of my journal, wrapping the leather strings around the cover. There had to be a better way for us, a way that didn't involve questions from strangers.

"No more paper," I finally said. "So, how are your eyes doing?"

He paused before wisdom tumbled down like boulders.

"My father used to say, 'There are none so blind as those who will not see.' But it wasn't until yesterday, until I had this surgery, that I understood the meaning of *will* not see, as opposed to *can* not see." His hand stroked his beard before resting underneath his chin. "Not only do I finally understand his statement, but now I understand the value of sight—and even more significant, of understanding and acting on this seeing."

I nodded furiously, grabbing the journal and pen from my bag again, pen trying its hardest to keep up. Now we were getting somewhere. The same proverb his father spoke traces its roots to a handful of different sources, most notably Jonathan Swift, Matthew Henry, and the Bible. Jeremiah 5:21 reads, "Hear this, you foolish and senseless people, who have eyes but do not see, who have ears but do not hear." According to the prophet, the Israelites were without understanding, "literally, without heart,"[3] and "willfully blind and obstinately deaf."[4] You certainly can't force someone to understand if they desire ignorance, and if, in their ability to see or hear, they will themselves unable to see or hear in the first place.

Taking a deep breath, I said a prayer of holy profundity. *Lord, give me the eyes to see, to really see.* I begged not to be without heart.

If James Meredith got to have his way the first day, I was determined to have my way the second. The first day, his eyes had finally given out after a couple of near misses in Judy's car. It was time for me to drive, but taking the wheel didn't mean I was in charge of our day. So when I arrived at the house the next morning and asked him if he was ready to go, he answered, "I am yours until you release me."

"What would you like to do today?" I asked, and he vehemently shook his head.

"I told you, I'm not in charge! You're in charge! And I am yours until you release me!" His direct, militaristic attitude exhausted me, but the smile on my face betrayed me: I couldn't help but love the man.

"Well, I'd like to go to the state capitol, to the museum that has a feature on you, and to Tougaloo College, if we have time," I replied, my words straight and to the point. *State the facts, ma'am, nothing but the facts,* I thought, certain my directness had been enough for his liking.

"Well, what are we waiting for?" He nodded toward the main road, fingers pointing as he yelled directions across the console. We would not be typing an address into Google Maps anytime soon, that much I knew.

Soon enough, we arrived at the Mississippi State Capitol, a darling of a building in the heart of downtown Jackson. His eyes were clearly feeling pain, he rubbed and dabbed and squeezed them tightly together. But a physical pain had spread to the rest of his body too: after we walked through the metal detector and made our way into the lobby of the rotunda, he all but fell into a nearby wheelchair.

I wheeled him to a leather bench underneath the marble staircase. In a few minutes, he'd be ready to give me a tour of the building. After all, his legacy haunted its walls: Two weeks before the integration, James Meredith, his lawyers, and several marshals made a second attempt to enroll him. Five days before that, Governor Ross Barnett, "bolstered by his sovereignty,"[5] appointed himself registrar for the University of Mississippi. When my father-in-law attempted to register for classes in the capitol building, Barnett and several state legislators physically blocked the Ole Miss officials, who *were* at that point willing to let him register. The racial hatred of the state had reached a whole new level, but not without a dash of Barnett's inept humor. After denying his admittance for the second time, the governor looked around the room and asked, "Which one is Meredith?" James Meredith, of course, was the only black man in the room.[6]

Four years later, another historic scene took place on the steps of the capitol building. Although President Johnson had passed the Voting Rights Act of 1965, an act that banned discriminatory practices meant to keep black voters away from the polls, my father-in-law saw how a stronghold of fear still gripped the black narrative of the southern states. So he embarked on a 220-mile walk, mostly by himself, a journey intended to take him from Memphis, Tennessee, down Highway 51 toward Jackson. But on the second day of the walk, white supremacist Aubrey James Norvell aimed a 16-gauge shotgun at my father-in-law. Norvell fired an estimated 450 shotgun pellets at him. Doctors later "dug as many as 70 pellets out of his scalp, back, limbs, even from behind an ear, before they questioned their effort"[7] and left the rest alone. News of the shooting spread to various leaders of the civil rights movement, including Martin Luther King Jr. and Stokely Carmichael, who began to walk on his behalf. Soon, a single man's walk turned into a fifteen-thousand-person nonviolent protest march for black voting rights, renamed the Meredith March Against Fear. Not only was it the largest civil rights demonstration in Mississippi's history, but it also birthed the Black Power movement.

I knew his stories lived in this place, just as I knew his legacy haunted its walls.

But first, he and I waited, and waited, and waited. And just as Bono sings in the modern-day rendering of the psalm, our insides cried out, "How long, how long, how long, how long to sing this song?"[8] How long to wait in the lobby of the state capitol? How long to take in Zenlike moments of peace instead of wheeling through history's halls? As the man in the wheelchair waited for me, I waited for him, my eyes glued to the colorful rotunda ceiling. In our silence we each waited for the other to take the lead.

"Well, are you ready to walk through the building?" I finally asked. Fifteen, twenty, thirty minutes must have gone by.

"Am I ready?" he shouted, his voice echoing through the chambers. "You slow! You slower than I thought! I just been waiting for you, girl!" He laughed as I grabbed the handles of the wheelchair and followed his direction toward the gold-colored elevator ten feet away.

Minus the occasional greeting from a secretary or porter, the capitol building was rather quiet with most of the staff away on summer vacation. We wheeled into the Senate House and parked in one corner of the room. I strolled around, snapping the occasional photograph and looking at portraits of past officials on the walls. That's when I saw it.

"Sir, why is the Confederate flag still being flown in the Mississippi State Capitol?"[9]

He nodded wearily, a southern *mmm-hmm* coming from his lips.

"That, my dear, is a very good question." But before he could answer, a senate porter walked into the room.

"Why, James Meredith! It's an honor and a pleasure to meet you, sir!" It's not uncommon for strangers to boldly walk up to a man they've esteemed all of their lives and thank him profusely. He is an emblem of hope in their eyes, an icon who changed the world with an unwillingness to give up the good fight.

"Why, it's an honor meeting you, Mr. Porter," he replied, over-come by amicability. "And do you know what my daughter-in-law just asked me? She asked me *why* the Confederate flag is still being flown in our great state." The three of us made our way toward a side room that doubled as a coffee and shoeshine room, and another porter joined us. The two African American men in their midfifties cozied up in the shoeshine chairs to listen as my father-in-law took center stage. He returned to my question and I returned to the place of observer.

"Why *is* the Confederate flag still being flown in our great state? It's this right here," he said, poking a finger into my arm. "And this right here," he added, leaning over to poke a pointer finger into the first porter's skin. "And if we can't get past that fact, we always gonna have problems. Until you get past the issue of black and white, or any other minority, you gonna have problems. So if we fail to address it, we gonna have problems."

A chorus of amens rose from our lips, reverberations of holiness echoing in the chambered room. But he wasn't done yet.

"And this woman right here? I made clear to her since she

married my son and had my grandbabies, only one thing is true: according to Mississippi state law, she no longer a white woman. She a black woman now! A black woman, you hear?"

"Yes!"

"Yes!" The voices of the men who sat in the shoeshine chairs rose up in unison.

"She too is bound by the chains of discrimination and hate. She too is tied to the problem, and until we address the problem of black and white, not a whole lot's gonna change. Not a whole lot's gonna change."

James Meredith finished his speech, hands swooping the air like a conductor's, his declaration the final note of his symphony. Our time here was done. Silence filled the coffee and shoeshine room, the scribbling of my pen the only sound any of us could hear. Looking up, I glanced around the room. There wasn't a dry eye in the place.

*L*ater that evening, I lay alone on the bed of my hotel room, my body heavy and still with weariness. Every part of me ached, the intensity of two days of conversation enough to fill a calendar year. This complicated, driven, unapologetic man had given me the gift of his time, a present intended not for me but for his grandsons. He and I weren't done growing in our relationship, but after spending a few days together, I finally felt like I'd tasted the problem that had plagued him every day of his life, the problem that drove him to push past fear and fight white supremacy in his home state. And one thing had become clear to me: his problem had become my problem too.

CHAPTER 13

Not Noticing

After my trip to Mississippi, I wanted nothing more than to be home with my boys. I wanted their wet, downy postbath curls against my chest and the clean scent of baby soap in my nostrils. I wanted to feel tiny human elbows and ribs and buns jockeying for comfort on my lap. I wanted to breathe in their littleness.

James and I usually volley back and forth when it comes to putting the boys in bed—*your turn, my turn, your turn, my turn*—but after I got back, they were all mine. When I sat down to read a couple of books with the boys, though, I couldn't help but notice a common theme: not a single character looked like my mixed-race sons. Except for Elephant and Piggie, an animal pair that starred in Theo's book of choice that night, every single character looked like me. Every single character was white with blonde or brunette hair.

"Why you stop reading, Mama?" Canon asked me.

"I think we're done reading this book, buddy." Tears welled in his eyes. I knew he saw it, even if he didn't recognize it in the moment, "it" being the blonde-haired, blue-eyed, pale-skinned children who sat at the feet of a brown-haired, brown-eyed, pale-skinned Jesus. Just as his ears listened to the rhyming intonation of the God who loved everyone in the toddler storybook Bible, his eyes saw a picture of who was in and who was out, a picture of those most welcomed at the feet of the Master. We did, of course, finish reading the story, but I tossed the book into the Goodwill pile the next morning. None of us needed to see that again.

"Am I overreacting?" I asked James later that night.

"You're not overreacting," he replied. "You're just noticing." I nodded: the privilege of not noticing had always been mine. I thought about the books I was drawn to, books written by white women memoirists who thought and believed and looked mostly like me. I thought about the dozens of theology books crammed onto the shelves of our home library, volumes of thoughts and facts about God written almost entirely by white men.

But when my boys snuggled into me and when my husband nestled into the crook of my arm, their malleable souls nestled into me too. When I visited my father-in-law and listened to him talk about the black and white problem in America, the problem crept into my soul. And when I began to let the names of the innocent, of those black and brown brothers and sisters who lost their lives to police brutality, become the words of my heart, I couldn't *not* notice anymore. Their stories became a part of me. Their stories helped me to look beyond my experiences. Their stories helped me to notice what I hadn't been reading and seeing all along, and their stories begged me to read the books and characters and authors I hadn't noticed in the first place.

I don't think it's any different for children. When every single book we read stars someone who looks more like me than my sons, something else is communicated: *This* is who rescues the bad guy. *This* is who dons the superhero cape. *This* is who wins in the end. When my sons see only a single skin color presented in the pages of a book, not only do they not see themselves but they digest a normalcy of supposed-to's, of who they are supposed to be and what they are supposed to look like. And in a Bible, of all things, when a message of whiteness replaces "the life and teachings of a dark-skinned first-century Jewish rabbi living under Roman occupation in Palestine,"[1] I am left with no choice but to wish the heartiest of farewells to this woefully defined image of the Christ.

Sometimes, though, the epiphany is harder than the reality. I pick my sons up from preschool one afternoon, determined to remedy our bookshelf situation.

"Who wants to go to the bookstore, boys?" Enthusiasm rolls off my tongue, making lemonade out of lemons.

"Me, me, me, me!" Canon exclaims.

"And me!" Theo echoes. They squeal about finding a book about the Paw Patrol, while I dream of discovering Caldecott Medal–winning literature that will guide us toward conversations of justice, of picture books with illustrations that mirror the faces of our family and of the world around us. It's hard to contain their excitement at the bookstore as we pull heavy wooden doors open and beeline to the children's section, to a place brimming with potential through the power of imagination.

I browse shelves of handwritten recommendations, of award-winning authors and illustrators, of brightly colored spines and front-facing covers splashed with blues and reds and greens, yellows and pinks and teals. Perhaps it doesn't come as much of a surprise to me that most of the books featuring children or authors of color are housed in a separate section labeled "diverse reading," further shouting of who's in and who's out, of what's normal and what's abnormal. According to one study, out of about 3,400 books analyzed, people of color accounted for only 22 percent of children's books characters.[2] While the number has more than doubled in two decades, I wonder what it means to read with intention, to look beyond the books I carelessly grab because I've read them in the past and am comfortable with them. I think about the books on their shelves and on my shelves too, and I wonder what it means to dig deeper and discover words that will change my perception, combat ignorance, and teach about the experiences of others.

As the boys litter the reading carpet with the glory of possibility, my mind wanders to authors like Toni Morrison and Maya Angelou, brilliant American writers whose works are highlighted not because they write about the black experience but because they swim circles around their white counterparts. I think about James Baldwin, whose words are just now beginning to seep into my soul, who also once wrote, "You think your pain and your heartbreak are unprecedented in the history of the world, but then you read."[3] He knew then, just as I'm learning now, that books connect us to the experiences of other people, of both the dead and those who are alive, to show us that we're not alone, to provide us with a sense of belonging.

As Canon and Theo clamber onto my lap, a book or two in each of their hands, my eyes scan the shelves of the children's section one last time. Just as I thought about the many books the boys and I had and hadn't read, I wondered about the many other places in my life I hadn't taken the time to notice. Where else hadn't I entered into tough conversations because I hadn't believed it to be my problem in the first place? Where had my lack of awareness caused another person pain because their narrative hadn't squarely fit into mine?

*S*ometimes the word privilege rolls off my tongue flippantly, defiantly, almost like a snarky version of my sixteen-year-old self. In truth, I've never had to think much about it.

I am a child of enough. Born into a white, middle-class American family, having enough is the only song I've ever sung, the only tune I've ever hummed. I may remember the occasional holiday with only one present underneath the Christmas tree, or the years when back-to-school shopping took place at the secondhand store, but we were not poor, not in the least. The system was still in our favor. I may remember the hours I studied and the papers I wrote, just as I remember the tuition checks I delivered to the business office every month in college and the credit card bill I racked up to pay for my seminary classes. Even though I worked hard, I still held the advantage of being ushered into higher education in the first place. After all, the American flag has always flown in my favor: every privilege, every right, every advantage, and every immunity my prerogative because of the color of my skin.

Privilege is a nest egg. Privilege is the family inheritance. Privilege is a trip to the Bahamas for Christmas and a vacation home in Boca Raton. Privilege is not worrying about where your next meal is going to come from because the pantry's always fully stocked. Privilege is defined as "a special right, advantage or immunity granted or available only to a particular person or group."[4] And this is where things can start to feel sticky, especially when our birth and our circumstances—things out of our control when we arrive on this earth—tell us that we are the recipients of "unearned social currency."[5] For many white people, this is also where the conversation quickly turns uncomfortable at best and threatening at worst. It feels like an attack. Every defensive bone in my body bristles in defense. It makes me feel guilty, like I *did* something to be born this way. Feelings of confusion overwhelm me, because how am I supposed to respond to something out of my control?

I returned from Mississippi to extreme August temperatures back home. The heat hit us all, but especially the boys.

"Mama, I'm hot," Canon squeaked from the top bunk.

"I know, buddy, I know. Just try to go to sleep." I sat in the chair a few feet away from him, squinting to read by the light of the late summer sun.

"Play, play?" Theo asked, sitting upright in a mountain of stuffed animals and blankets.

"No, baby, no play. It's time to go to sleep." I couldn't blame either one of them: I wouldn't have wanted to try to sleep while it was still light out or as hot as Hades either. Theo began singing every other syllable of "You Are My Sunshine" as Canon tried to wrestle his thoughts into nocturnal submission.

"Okay, come on, guys, sleep is a privilege. Let's do this." My words surprised me: how and why had I equated privilege with sleep? Perhaps it was because I never seemed able to sleep through the night. For two and a half years, I sprang awake right around two o'clock every morning, plagued by excruciating back pain and an inability to fall back to sleep. Pregnancy-related, one doctor said. Weight-related, another advised. Chiropractors called it the result of a herniated disk; massage therapists, the result of breastfeeding; acupuncturists, the early signs of arthritis inflammation. James and I bought a new mattress, but I ended up on the couch most nights, popping tablets of Ibuprofen and praying the heating pad might provide some relief. Maybe sleep really is a privilege after all.

"What's privilege, Mama?" Canon asked, his *r* sounding more like a *w*, *l* more like a *y*.

"Well, buddy, that's a good question. It's kind of like a right," I finally said, but I knew my definition didn't do the word justice.

In an article for *Relevant* magazine, Jemar Tisby defines privilege as "possessing certain traits that are considered more desirable in a certain community and thus, give a person easy access to the rewards of the community."[6] In that way, privilege goes beyond race, extending to gender, wealth, sexuality, education, and religion, to name a few, and particularly as it relates to race, "white privilege doesn't mean your life isn't hard. It means that if you are a person of color, simply by virtue of that, your life might be harder."[7]

Those of us who identify as white can choose not to notice. And that freedom doesn't end there. We can choose to ignore the social issues of people of color, remaining largely unaffected ourselves. We can be assumed trustworthy when we walk through the aisles of a department store, not followed around by a store manager or by security. We can head directly to the first-aid aisle of the neighborhood drugstore and have no trouble finding suitably colored bandaids for our skin. We are rarely asked to speak on behalf of our entire racial group. And we won't be accused of pulling out the race card if we publicly worry or fret over issues of race.[8]

Oftentimes, this is where the conversation both begins and ends, at least for those who identify as white. This is where defensiveness sets in and anger begins. This is the place where a fellow human being feels attacked for something entirely out of his or her control.

And this is the place where we forget to tune our ears and listen to another side of the story, a side of the story that isn't about us.

*W*ithin a couple of weeks, James and I found ourselves in front of the television: him in the comfy paisley chair, me stretched out on the leather couch. A recap of Sunday's football games flashed on the screen, and for once in my life, I lay enthralled by the scene before me: following disheartened tweets from the forty-fifth president, the Associated Press reported on the more than 130 NFL players, coaches, and owners kneeling, linking arms, and staying behind in locker rooms during the performance of the "The Star-Spangled Banner."

"Love, tell me more about what this means!" I exclaimed, hopeful for any tidbits he could give me.

"I guess Christmas Day has come a little early this year," he replied, a wry grin across his face. James was thinking not about a bounty of gifts on December 25 but about the hope that accompanies the season, made present in a tiny baby. A new confidence birthed within him when he saw players, coaches, and owners taking a stand in unity for their black and brown teammates. But then his brow furrowed, lightness erased. "Something needed to be done, but this may not be the most effective way to bring attention to the situation."

"Why? Because people will see it as political?"

"Well, sure. I mean, instead of highlighting the social and economic injustices borne mainly by African Americans in this country, people see it as disrespecting the military servicemen and women who fought for this country."

"So what else could we do?"

"I think if we knew how to solve the problem of race in our country, we wouldn't be having this conversation." There was no denying the man is his father's son.

As James reminded me, kneeling in protest wasn't anything new. During the 2016 season, former professional quarterback Colin Kaepernick championed against inequities in the criminal justice system by kneeling during the national anthem: "I am not going to stand up to show pride in a flag for a country that oppresses black people and people of color. To me, this is bigger than football and it would be selfish on my part to look the other way. There are bodies in the street and people getting paid to leave and getting away with murder."[9] Twitter roared with negative reaction. Football fans from around the country booed his act of protest. Critics from around the globe pointed fingers at the young, mixed-race man, eventually voting him the most disliked player in the NFL. By kneeling, he had singlehandedly disrespected the American flag, the US military, and the entire country, naysayers declared, the president included. But nearly a year later, with racial tensions at an all-time high, entire teams followed Kaepernick's lead, not in disrespect of the United States but in reverent respect for the lives of their black and brown brothers and sisters.

Both in the living room that afternoon and alone in my office a couple of mornings later, I stood in the middle of all of the shouting and all of the yelling. I wanted to press my hands over my ears and squeeze my eyes shut like a small child: *if I can't see the hate and I can't hear the hate, then the hate can't see me!* If I could somehow remain immune to the pain, then I wouldn't feel its effects.

Though I'm not a sportswriter or even a regular sports viewer, I saw enough to know that somehow, in the midst of trying to prove who was right and who was wrong (and, in the Christian world, of trying to prove whose version of Jesus was the holiest and most authentic of all), many Americans forgot about the humanity at the center. Even though there might be a better way forward, as James surmised, this wasn't about the flag, nor was it about not respecting the many women and men who've sacrificed their lives in performing their duty to our country.

I thought about a conversation I'd had with my dad only a week or two earlier. He and I sat across from one another at a coffee shop, matching glasses of iced tea on the table before us. I had interviewed nearly every one of my family members for my book in an effort to hear their stories and better understand my own. But when it came time to ask him the set of questions I'd asked everyone else, I hesitated. Glancing at the worn piece of paper the questions were on, it seemed they almost ran together, ink spilling across wrinkled lines of typeface: "What are some of your earliest memories of race and ethnicity?" "What did the culture around you communicate when it came to issues of race and justice?" "What comes to mind when you hear phrases like 'white privilege' and 'affirmative action'?" I wondered whether this was really the best way to engage my dad in the conversation, especially when we didn't see eye to eye on it, but I also didn't know where else to start.

Especially in my twenties, the more I learned at school and from the world around me, the more my opinions changed. And the more my opinions changed, the more I believed it my right to voice my thoughts wherever I pleased, to whomever I pleased. But with my dad, when my grown-up beliefs began to differ from my childhood beliefs, it became more important for me to win the argument than to think through how he might best receive a conversation. As I sat in the coffee shop that day, I felt my heartbeat quicken within me, palms suddenly sweaty as I waited for his answer.

"Dad, what comes to your mind when you hear the phrase 'white privilege'?" I asked. I could feel his anger rising. This was one of those dinner-table conversations that made me want to return to the days of snuggling up to him on the overstuffed couch while he gave the world's greatest performance of *Tom Sawyer*, the one no one but our family would ever see. I knew my question would feel like an attack on his personhood. And I was right.

"I personally am insulted by it, because I was never given white privilege," he finally replied. "I put myself through college; my dad didn't even help me. I earned a GI Bill and it took me ten years to pay off the loans I accrued after the bill ran out. As far as I know, I never displaced or was hired over anybody else because of the color of my skin. So I'm not saying it doesn't happen, it just didn't happen to me."

I nodded, glancing up at him when he finished speaking. This was the answer I had anticipated. But this was not the time for arguing, nor was it the time to tell him everything that white privilege entails. No amount of iced tea could soothe the parched divide between us, between a father and daughter who equally thirsted for the other person to understand.

I paused, unsure how to proceed, desperate for him to believe my love for him, even if we disagreed.

"So, Dad," I finally said, "how do we solve the issues of race and privilege in America today?"

"God is the only way forward," he said, a new boldness about him. "Right now, I am reading the Bible in a year. I am absolutely amazed, because I've never done this before. I've never read the Bible entirely through. But I am amazed at how patient God was with the Israelites, how he was always willing to help them when they cried out to him. God has infinite patience. He's used it on me, and he's used it on all of us, so the least I can do is be as patient as I can."

"Even in matters of race and privilege, when you don't agree with what I'm saying?" I asked.

"Maybe. But that might be taking it too far."

"Agreed."

"Are we done here?" he asked, tiredness overcoming him. This was not the easiest conversation, not for him and not for me. But we were entering into dialogue nonetheless. We were practicing patience and seeking understanding with one another, maybe for the first time in a long time. We were trying to be grown-ups with each other, even if we disagreed. I stared at the melted ice at the bottom of our plastic cups, lids thrown to the side as our teeth crunched on watered-down cubes. We really were more alike than different. A stillness of solidarity filled the moment: we might not be able to change one another's minds, but we can still seek to hear each other's hearts. We can still believe in change and in the ways our opinions and beliefs can evolve over time—I'd seen this in him and in myself. And when we camped out on this commonality, somehow it made us honor the human in one another, daughter to father, woman to man, human to human.

*M*aybe learning to listen and seeking to honor the humanity in one another is all that matters in the end. But when I witnessed a bunch of players and coaches kneeling for a song I hadn't ever thought was wrong, I wondered what prompted Kaepernick to kneel in the first place.

I could sing the first verse of "The Star-Spangled Banner" with my eyes closed, and had heard the second verse once or twice over the years. But the third verse of the song was new to me:

> No refuge could save the hireling and slave
> From the terror of flight or the gloom of the grave,
> And the star-spangled banner in triumph doth wave
> O'er the land of the free and the home of the brave.[10]

At first glance, the interpretation seems obvious: if nothing can save a slave from death, then the poem celebrates the murder of African Americans. Francis Scott Key, a slaveholder himself, opposed the abolition of slavery; during the War of 1812, he penned the anthem after the British invaded Fort McHenry, nearly twenty years before the abolitionist movement began.

Some historians speculate that "the gloom of the grave" refers not to imminent, literal death but to a metaphorical death of slave ownership in the United States, when the British recruited (and refused to give back to their American owners) more than six thousand slaves at the time of the invasion. Others say that the meaning of the word slave is different to contemporary ears, not connoting human chattel, per se, and not referring to the most oppressed of ethnic groups forced into slave labor, African Americans.[11] "At the time Key was writing, the word 'slave' . . . had long functioned in English as a wide-ranging epithet, hurled at persons of any and all colors, nationalities, and conditions of servitude or otherwise," states Walter Olson of the *National Review*.[12] If this is true, then Key could have been referring to involuntary conscripts on the British side of the war and not to the black slaves he himself owned.

Regardless of Key's intention (an intention I believe included the mistreatment of African Americans), if the song feels racially hostile to those who have lived under the reign of oppression for more than four hundred years in their home country, then it *is* an expression of racial hostility. In my privilege—including advantages of skin color, wealth, and education—I can choose whether Key's poem qualifies as racist because my experience allows me to dismiss all racism, courtesy of a single commentary written in my favor. After all, mine is a privilege born of entire systems designed to work for people who look like me. Mine is a privilege that allows me to step in and out of conversations of race, of racial injustice, and of the social problems of people of color. Mine is a privilege that doesn't have to think much about the history I was taught, because it came from the mouths of people who look and think like me.

But I can choose a different way of noticing and listening. I can tune my ears to hearing a new song. Closing my eyes, I can let new rhythms and melodies make room in my soul, just as I can allow new sounds of harmony and dissonance to build a house in my heart. And just as this great symphony begins to swirl around in my blood, it changes me from the inside out. It gives me permission to honor the experiences of my fellow human beings, in all the ways we are the same and in all the ways we are different from one another too. Dancing to a new beat that pulses from my head all the way down to my toes, I beg for more, desperate to notice the sounds I haven't heard before.

CHAPTER 14

A Beautiful Both-And

*C*anon sprawled across the kitchen floor, marker in hand, the weight of his body bent over a piece of construction paper.

"Mama," he asked, "how do you spell, 'I wish I had dark skin'?" He looked up at me in innocence as tears sprang up in my eyes. One by one, I spelled the words he wanted to know; one by one, he drew a box around each word, black lines as thick as the space between words. Someday he would not separate the words on a page with boxes, but first, this.

I leaned into the kitchen counter. He and I would leave in a few minutes so I could preach, the occasional Sunday morning guest sermon part of my ministry, part of my job. *Mama is going to talk to the grown-ups this morning. Can you be a good listener, buddy?* With James and Theo away on a daddy-son adventure, it was just the two of us. But when Canon said those words, I put my notes to the side. I stopped staring at the text in front of me and closed my Bible. This could wait. It all could wait. Spelling out the words written on his heart was all that mattered.

There are a handful of people who matter most to my son, starting with his brother, his mother, and his father. He has a best friend named Ben but is quick to tell you that he's friends with everyone in his class. He rattles off the names of his cousins, his aunties and his uncles, and the grandparents on both sides: Gaga and Papa, Nana and Granddaddy. As he's gotten older, he has grown in awareness of the color of his skin. Mama has light skin. Daddy has dark skin. Canon and Theo are clothed in a mixture of light and dark, with fine, curly hair to boot. When he makes a declaration of skin color and realizes that he is neither black nor white, neither European American nor African American, my lament springs from knowing he already feels caught between two worlds. The underpinnings of division, of feeling like you don't fully belong in either place, have already caught up with him—so much so, I would guess, that it makes him want not to have to choose.

I sat down on the kitchen floor, legs spread out before me.

"Hey, buddy, come here for a second," I finally said, pulling him toward my chest. "You are a pretty special dude, you know that, right?" He nodded, eyes wide with a knowledge already held in his heart.

"And part of what makes you special is that you're a mix of Mama and Daddy. You are black and white: not just black and not just white but a perfect combination of the two. Does that make sense?" Again, he nodded his head, maybe thinking about the books we'd read about mixed-race children just like him, or maybe connecting the dots to previous conversations we'd stumbled through in the dinner hour.

"But I know it's hard to feel like you're in the middle, like you live in a world of in-between, not just like Mama and not just like Dada. So I'm sorry if that makes you feel sad. I sure don't like it when you feel sad." He looked up at me, pen in one hand and paper in the other.

"Love you, Cancan."

"Love you, Mama," he squeaked back. Hoisting one another up, we got ready to leave.

*M*ixed-race children have long stood at the center of public and private debates in American culture, taking center stage midway through the twentieth century. In *Brown v. Board of Education of Topeka,* the state of Kansas claimed integration was a slippery slope: "if black children were allowed in schools, all sorts of terrible things would happen."[1] As with my father-in-law's integration, the argument against integration included the implication that mixed-race children would result: if schools are integrated, then black children and white children will mix, inside and outside of the classroom. When they mix outside of the classroom, they will fall in love; when they fall in love, they will have sex; when they have sex, they will repopulate the earth with their black and white "spawn."[2]

The same thing happened less than a decade later in *Loving v. Virginia* when the state's argument centered on the premise that mixed marriages would have a horrible impact on the children born to those marriages.[3] Although Richard and Mildred Loving ultimately won, fear continued in the hearts of many Americans, a fear not just of blacks mixing with whites but of the byproduct of interracial mixing: the children. Across America, the public feared what they did not know, what they could not understand. As a result, they pieced together the only truths the past could tell, truths that extended into my life as well.

"Cara," my mama once said to me, "you know we'll accept any man you bring home. But if you marry a black man, I'll worry about your children. I wouldn't want them to have to choose between races." Her fear was rooted in words passed down to her: in the early seventies, before she met my father, she dated a black man. They got each other. They shared the same sense of humor and the same taste in music, the same group of bell-bottomed, dreadlocked friends, and the same love of Napa Valley wine. But they did not share a vision of the children they could have brought into this world. "It's a sentiment of choice," she remembers him saying to her. Not wanting their potential kin to have to choose between two ethnic identities, he broke up with her.

Taking his words to heart, she passed them along to me, even if it was a truth rooted in a fear of not knowing, a fear of having to choose, a fear of being caught in the middle. Later, after meeting her future son-in-law, long before procreation even entered the conversation, she apologized to me, never mentioning her warning again. Were we to have children, she would love them with abandon, and her pursuit of love for her grandchildren has never faltered since the boys came into all our lives. Unlike many interracial couples who have had to navigate severed familial relationships as a result of their union, healing has found its way into parts of our story, including the stories of those closest to us. But sometimes the hauntings and the questions remain, long into marriage and throughout the early years of parenthood. Before the poppy seeds of human life began growing in my body, I wondered whether this would be the case for us, whether our children would feel caught between two worlds, between different cultures and ethnicities. Just as the states of Kansas and Virginia and everyone else seemed to argue, would our children struggle to find their racial identities? As they grew older, what would whiteness and blackness, including the whiteness of Mama and the blackness of Daddy, mean to them?

Maybe that's when my real prayers began, when the "help, thanks, wow" instructions of Anne Lamott wiggled their way into my heart.[4] Help, God: you've given me the eyes to see the beauty of your world, in all its color, in all its glory, in all its pain. Thanks, God: you've put a desire to learn in my heart and in my mind. Might I use it for good, especially when it comes to showing empathy toward those who feel like they live in an in-between world of black and white. Wow, God: you're really something else. You've outdone yourself this time, allowing my heart to live outside my body, in the skin and bones of my sons. How'd I get so lucky to be their mama?

After all, sometimes life is just one big series of awakenings, one after another after another. You wake up to the world around you, to the things you didn't know yesterday but hope to know today. You wake up to a reality of present pain, to hurts you hadn't known existed a month before. And you wake up to seeing that your viewpoint is not the center of the universe; you see that there might be another way of thinking, of living, of existing different from what you've always thought. So you acknowledge and you dig into the hardships of your past—of your people by blood and your people by citizenship—but you do not let that keep you from moving forward.

You press on, with hope.

And you keep putting one foot in front of the other. Sometimes walking forward and sometimes taking a step or two backward, but always, always, by keeping your heart in motion.

A year and a half after Theo was born, life got crazy. I felt like I'd spent the previous eighteen months with my head buried in the sand, limbs and legs flailing from side to side, up and down, and back again. But then I started to dig myself out of the sand. Keeping two small humans alive got easier, and just as we tend to say to each other in the midst of struggle, "it gets easier" became a true mantra. Life wasn't perfect by any stretch of the imagination, but it did get easier when Theo turned one and didn't need my body for sustenance any longer. It did get easier when both boys learned how to walk without my holding their tiny hands every step of the way. It did get easier when, after moving from one side of the Bay Area to the other, we found a support system of friends who seemed to speak the same language and want the same things. And it did get easier when James and I took the time to sit on a couch together, the listening ears of a therapist a shield between us.

James craved the warmth of physical touch. I needed the support of a partner, both in parenting and in my writing career. And we both needed someone to validate the constant, changing nature of our relationship: we met, we married, we had our first child, and then a second. He changed jobs. I left my job. We moved multiple times, up and down the Peninsula and over to the East Bay. We found our people, we lost our people, and we found our people again. As we looked at our list of changes, a bounty of tumult in less than four years, it was about time we sat down on her couch. The many transitions that marked our young marriage were a lot for one person to take in, let alone for the two of us to navigate without a trained counselor. But a funny thing happened during our time on the couch: we realized that we hadn't taken the time—nor had we *had* the time—to think about how our individual stories of race, culture, and ethnicity tied in to the greater story of the two of us, of our sons, and of the world around us. So the therapist gave us some homework.

"Write this down. Read everything you can get your hands on about whiteness, about blackness, about race and culture. Write your way through the stories of your racial and cultural contexts, if you haven't already. And Cara, this one's for you: come to the session I'm leading in a couple of months on the experience of being mixed. I think it'll be particularly helpful for you as a mother of mixed-race children." I nodded, nervous and excited about the journey we would enter, but I knew that with every step forward, I would also take at least two, if not two thousand, steps backward.

Zealous in my pursuit to put pen to paper, I began exploring my thoughts in various online writing portals. Call it the curse of writing in the twenty-first century, but the fact that my writing journey could be private instead of public hadn't really crossed my mind.

When an editor asked me if I would write a letter to my mixed-race sons, I jumped at the chance. I was eager to get my name out there. I believed the world needed to hear a mother's perspective of what it means to feel like you're both-and and neither-nor all at the same time. When "A Letter to My Black Son—With Love from Your White Mama"[5] ran, it oozed sentimentality. I wrote the piece in less than an hour while Theo took an afternoon nap and Canon watched two and a half reruns of *Curious George*. And when that happens to a writer, when the words pour out of you, quick like liquid gold, you know you've said exactly what you're supposed to say. You know you've spoken the truest words within you, for you've unearthed a story hidden in the marrow of your bones.

> Dear Baby Boy,
>
> You don't see it now, because you don't see color. But someday you will. Someday you will look around you at the kids in your class and your friends and church, and you will realize that you don't look like them. Your skin is a little bit lighter than the girl standing to your right, and a little bit darker than the boy sitting to your left. And then someday you will be asked to check the box marked "ethnicity" or "race," and you won't know what to choose. You will think about your father, who is black, and you will think about your mother, who is white, and you will wonder what color you are, you will wonder which box you should choose.
>
> And that might make you mad. It might make you sad. It might make you feel like you don't belong, like you live in an in-between space, in a place that doesn't feel very fair.
>
> Well, my love, I want to tell you something: You are a most beautiful *both-and* who most definitely belongs.
>
> You are black and you are white, and that makes you the

most gorgeous, drinkable shade of caramel cappuccino. So check both of those boxes if you want to, if you need to, if that's what you think should happen. Pencil them in with pride.

For you need not ever feel or be ashamed of the color of your skin. You are perfect, just as you are.

The letter continued, talking about how I oftentimes felt inadequate as a white woman in the fight against racism, before wholeheartedly resolving to continue fighting until the bitter end. God's stamp on humanity was worth it all. My words were the stuff of Hallmark movies, I thought: heartwrenching, soul clenching, a crackle of fire within. But then I did something at the very end, something I knew I didn't need to do but also knew would shake up my audience and draw attention to my words: I ended the letter by calling him my handsome black boy. For nearly 850 words, I highlighted the realities and the hardships, the joys and the pains of living in mixed-race skin, and then, in an effort to drive more traffic, I negated the message with a single word. I called him black. I did what I knew I wasn't supposed to do—what none of us are supposed to do—and labeled him according to what *I* saw on the outside, ignoring his choice of identity. Even if Theo, who has darker skin, whose baby face I pictured as I wrote the letter, does someday identify as a black man, the qualifier wasn't mine to make. This identifier, this label, this proclamation of "black" is not mine to make, not now and not ever.

*S*oon after the letter published, with accolades and criticism still dogging my heels, I drove over the Bay Bridge to attend the workshop led by our therapist. Staring at the reflection of water in the glass of the skyscrapers, I thought about the stranger who reached out to warn me about adding the word black at the end of the letter. A mother of mixed-race children herself, she knew the grave danger of getting the conversation wrong. But I also thought about those readers who reached out to say thank you, to tell me that until the letter posted, they hadn't thought about living with a both-and identity, about what it must be like to live in mixed-race skin. Maybe this comes with the territory, I thought. Some people will like what I have to say, and some people won't. Sometimes I'll get it right and sometimes I'll get it wrong, and when that happens, I'll learn to show myself grace before gearing up to start all over again. I'll learn to say, over and over again, "I'm sorry. I'm listening. Keep talking," for I can never stop leaning into the voices who have gone before me. But I'll also vow not to neglect my responsibility to just do something, because when it comes to conversations of race and injustice, it's my job to figure out what that something is and to let that something lead to even more somethings.[6] That day, my something involved taking notes until my hand cramped and learning from a couple of therapists who had something to teach me.

My therapist and another woman, who both identified as mixed-race, led a forty-five minute presentation titled "On the Experience of Being Mixed: A Juxtaposition of Pride and Shame."[7] Although I wasn't a therapist (nor would I likely ever choose to pursue work as a therapist, bless their listening souls), the California Association of Marriage and Family Therapists granted me permission to attend the single session. There weren't more than a dozen or so people in the room. But that didn't stop their presentation from having its intended impact, my mind brimming over with thoughts for and about my sons.

"When it comes to counseling mixed individuals," one of the therapists said, "you have to understand what it's like when someone asks, 'What are you?' Mixed individuals are always then asking,

'Where do I fit?' They want to fit in one or the other group, but how do they gain access, especially when society *wants* to plug you in to one of two groups?" I suppose we Americans like our boxes, wanting to put those who identify as mixed-race into a single box that makes sense in our minds. We like the security of knowing how and where our little slice of the world fits with the images we've so perfectly created. Without knowing it, we compartmentalize humanity, organizing others and even ourselves with labels that fit our understanding of the world. Some of us do this in our faith traditions, putting God into a box of comfortable systems of religion and right relationships. It's not any wonder that we do the same thing with ethnic identity, making assumptions of those our eyes can't quite nail down, squeezing the outside of their bodies into boxes of our understanding. But now that nearly half of mixed-raced Americans are younger than eighteen, it's imperative that we do better (besides the fact that it's not our job to define and put a box around another person's racial identity in the first place). Once again, I realized I had a responsibility to do my homework: just as I had to deconstruct the singular way I viewed the world when it came to issues of race, I had to break down notions of racial identity when it came to raising my sons.

An image of the past floated through my mind: I was sixteen years old, a student leader at a weekend retreat for the nonprofit organization I would later work for as an adult. A couple dozen of us lounged across the hardwood living room floor, a marker and piece of construction paper before each one of us.

"Who are you?" our director bellowed from the front, his face exuberant as he raised a pointer finger from person to person across the room. I knew we weren't supposed to answer his question out loud, but that didn't stop my fingers from itching with the desire to answer it. He pointed to a large, hand-drawn picture of a shield broken into four quadrants on a white board beside him, and instructed us to draw the same: across the top, we were to write the words, "Who am I?" and label each space with the words "Me," "Family," "Friends," "God." I remember filling the space with different facts of my personality and my personhood: *optimistic, musical, friend to everyone, sister and daughter, loves Jesus!* I filled the spaces of the shield with every word I could think of to describe my adolescent self, the myriad ways I interacted with my family and with the world around me. But nowhere did I write about my racial identity, about how my siblings and I were both Ashkenazi Jews and Northwestern Europeans, a mixture of our Jewish, Scottish, and Irish ancestors. I didn't write about the heritages and cultures of those who came before me because that part of my identity didn't matter to me. As a teenager, I didn't question where I fit into society because as a white person, mine was the dominant experience in the world around me.

But I knew this wasn't the case anymore, especially not after that morning with Canon in the kitchen. No longer could I remain at a safe, comfortable distance from this part of my son's identity, because this magical, delicate combination of his humanity as a mixed-race boy lived at the core of his existence. It was up to me to do diligence, to dig in to understanding what it feels like to live as a perpetual foreigner and an outsider, like "you cannot choose either side because you are not merely one of your two halves—you are both, and you are neither."[8] It was up to me to read as many books and articles as I could get my hands on, just as it was on me to listen to the stories of those who identified as multiracial, to hold both the tragedy and the beauty of living in neither-nor skin. "I am a mongrel, a mutt, a half-breed, a Heinz 57," one woman wrote. "I'm mulatto, biracial, mixed. I am all of these things and none of these things."[9] Although these friends owed me nothing, I knew I owed them a listening ear, even if I wondered whether I would ever feel the full weight of their disorientation.

But I could try, so try I did. My eyes glazed over reading lists of slurs on the Racial Slur Database, wholly ignorant of the more than 120 slurs given for mixed race persons. I wondered if doing my homework meant digging into words like "mulatto," "NASA" (North American Street Ape), and "quadroon," words that didn't make me feel warm and gushy inside but nonetheless caused me to raise my awareness of racism.[10]

I texted James after reading studies like one from the University of Edinburgh that claimed that in a study of more than 350,000 people, those who identified as mixed-race were on average 1.2 centimeters taller and had nearly an additional year of formal education than their peers who had parents of similar genetic makeups.[11] "What do you think? Is it true?" I asked my husband. "Random coincidence?" he replied. I hadn't yet read about the controversy within those kinds of studies: all of that would come with time. For now, I simply had a responsibility to listen and learn.

As I read articles that made me squeal in one breath and squirm in the next, I also learned that individuals who are mixed-race not only have access to more cultures and communities than they would within a single cultural context but they oftentimes have a greater ability to move within multiple people groups. One man wrote, "The interesting thing about being multiracial is that when you stand out from the mainstream, you kind of fit in everywhere,"[12] while another woman saw her mixed-race heritage as a wealth because "it opens your mind and it makes you more tolerant because you know by your own experience that sometimes it can be difficult and tricky."[13] Especially as children grow older, mixed-race persons are able to address differences and find doors into the problems in their worlds. Recognizing one another's strengths, they possess an uncanny knack for sharing stories, because in realizing the many layers of their own stories, they recognize the layers in *every* story, including the stories I might easily dismiss.

The research brought to mind stories different mixed-race people had shared with me. Through a friend, I met Shane, a young mixed-race man who identifies as black. "Sometimes I laugh when I say, 'As a black man . . .' I completely understand the fact that my mom is white and that I'm half-white. But that's not necessarily how other people see me, nor is it how I identify myself,"[14] he said, a slight smile on his face. Shane's racial identity primarily comes from how other people see him: he will always see himself as a black man, mostly because he will never be able to identify as a white man. But he doesn't see that as a bad thing, not in the least.

Likewise, Teylar, an executive assistant in Seattle, Washington, admitted that being a mixed-race African American and European American person can be tricky, because two different things don't always easily fit together.[15] But as she continues to identify with her black heritage, piecing together parts of her personal narrative, she finds solace in knowing the end of the story, when in the book of Revelation,[16] God lives among the people. People from all nations and tribes and tongues come together to worship at the mountain of hope, and although they are different from one another, they have been created with intention.

"Why would God create intentionally, if God didn't care about the intentional things that make up me?" As Teylar posed this question to me, images of my sons flashed through my mind: God saw them and honored their multiracial identities, not in spite of but because of the particularities of their personhood. And maybe that's when it hit me: at the end of the day, all I wanted was wholeness, for my boys and for myself, for my husband and for a world full of hurting people around us. I could rattle off a list of statistics about how population change favors minorities, that by 2042, minorities will make up 54 percent of the US population,[17] or that in a couple of years "more than half of all children will be minorities."[18] While these statistics *do* count for something, when it came to my children, all I wanted was for wholeness to seep out of their souls.

In Hebrew, wholeness is at the root of the word *shalom*. Defined as "a covenantal theology of wholeness," shalom has five variations: well-being, wholeness, perfection of God's creation, abundance, and peace.[19] Shalom, I read, is the goal. Shalom is the persistent vision. Shalom is "the freight of a dream of God that resists all our tendencies to division, hostility, fear, drivenness, and misery,"[20] but it doesn't end there. "Shalom is God's dream for his love to bring wholeness and goodness to the world and everything within it, including you and me."[21] Just as shalom is the presence of the goodness of God, shalom is the presence of wholeness and completeness.[22] Shalom is who we were meant to be and how we were meant to operate in this world. Without a doubt, this dripping, oozing, dribbling wholeness was all I really wanted for my sons.

A week or so after the moment in the kitchen, the four of us hunkered down for a Saturday morning together. We took our time at home, not rushing to get anywhere, eating waffles with peanut butter and extra syrup together as a family. Canon and Theo played in the playroom off the side of the kitchen, a space intended as a breakfast nook but ideal for zooming trucks, building railroad tracks, and creating towers of stuffed animals. James sipped his coffee. I read my book. Without looking at the clock, the two of us sensed it was time to wriggle out of pajamas and get dressed. We stuffed reusable bags into the bottom of the stroller and walked four blocks down the hill to the farmer's market and the adjacent playground.

"Hey, buddy, want to taste an apple?"

"Theo, would you like a bite of beef jerky?"

"Love, look! They have our favorite sourdough bread!" At the market, we took pleasure in the free samples, making sure to stop by my favorite vegetable stand, the one with a two-pound bag of mixed greens, topped with a rainbow of edible flowers. James stood in line: salmon tacos for him, a vegetarian chimichanga with extra salsa for me. Two booths down, another waffle, this one with butter and powdered sugar for the boys.

Eventually, we found our way to the center of the market, crowding to the front where a reggae band jammed on a makeshift stage. Canon's elbows drifted upward and hung midair, like an old man: right elbow up, left elbow up, knee up, knee down, booty out, repeat. His body glided in motion to the beat of the music, his insides created for movement, for dance, for expression. James mimicked his moves, throwing in a Michael Jackson spin of his own, his grown man's feet gliding over the bricks of the square. Theo raised his arms for me to pick him up. My left arm cupped his bottom while my right hand reached for his tiny hand. My baby and I moved in sync to the music, a classical dancer's pose reinvented for mother and son, ours an outdoor party in the middle of a city park.

I looked around the space, awed by the explosion of diversity in the world around me, transfixed by the three I called my own. Throwing my head back in laughter, I continued in our made-up dance, and for once, I stopped trying to figure it all out in my mind. Struggle would inevitably come, that much I knew, because for now, my boys knew love and acceptance, wholeness theirs in the midst of their fully black and fully white selves.

CHAPTER 15

We, Ours, Us

"A re they yours?" a young woman asked me, staring at me and then at the boys, eyes darting back and forth between us. My entire body was engaged in a dance of the swings. I pushed Theo in the baby swing before doing a little hop, skip, and jump to the right to push Canon in the big kid swing. Back and forth I went, dancing on asphalt. I looked at her and smiled.

"Yup," I replied. "They're all mine." This wasn't the first time a stranger had attempted to make conversation on the playground, nor was it the first time someone had tried to give order to the puzzle in his or her mind.

"So did you adopt them, or are they, like, biologically yours?"

I cringed. "You mean, did I grow them in my body? Yes, I grew them in my body. They came from me. I am not the babysitter. My husband is a black man. We have mixed-race kids." I was done with the conversation and we both knew it. Usually, I don't mind talking to strangers, especially when the conversation involves a topic I am most passionate about: my children. The very definition of a proud mama hen, I can gab about them for hours, even when someone wants to understand how we fit together when we don't look all that much alike.

Her questions, of course, weren't new. Just days before, when my friend Julie and I stood in line together at preschool pickup, she told me about being the mother of biracial children. "I've been asked three times if I'm the nanny," she said, looking through the glass partition at her daughter. "I've been asked in other ways if I'm the biological mom, what they're mixed with, what race my husband is. The nanny thing always catches me off guard and offends me every time I'm asked. I mean, no one's outright saying anything racist, but, well, they're racist."[1] Julie, a white woman, and her husband, Kwasi, a first-generation Ghanaian American, have two mixed-race daughters. But it wasn't until her daughters were born that a fair amount of noticing began. I wonder if it wasn't all that different for me.

That day on the playground, though, the woman's questions felt more like an accusation than a desire to understand. Although my boys and I do not look the same on the outside, the intimate details of who they are and how they got here and who *I* am to them were not hers to know in the first place, even though a snarky part of me did answer some of her questions.

The stranger walked away without a word, her mouth agape. I wondered if I should feel bad. I wondered if I should beg God for forgiveness and mercy and patience. But instead, I just continued my dance of the swings.

*M*ost of the time, graciousness *is* my response, or at least the response I hope to have with strangers on the playground. I knew she was probably just trying to make small talk or thought my sons were the most adorable human beings ever seen swinging on a pint-sized swingset. Even more, her own lonely human self just wanted to connect with another lonely human self. But for me, the weight of the week's events didn't allow for such grace, at least not in that moment.

Days earlier, a grand jury decided not to prosecute the two police officers involved in the shooting death of twelve-year-old Tamir Rice. Even though the boy's murder was caught on camera, even though the person who called 911 stated twice that the gun was *probably* a fake and that the person holding the gun was *probably* a juvenile, and even though the entire incident happened in less than two seconds, the grand jury ruled there was insufficient evidence. Instead, they issued the following declaration: "Given this perfect storm of human error, mistakes and communications by all involved that day, the evidence did not indicate criminal conduct by police."[2] The City of Cleveland reprimanded the two officers, Timothy Loehmann and Frank Garmback, as well as the 911 dispatcher who neglected to pass along critical information from the caller. Although the police force placed both men on administrative leave, they eventually fired Loehmann, who had neglected to disclose a previous evaluation that labeled him an emotionally unstable recruit unfit for duty.[3] The city also settled a lawsuit for six million dollars, awarding money to the mother and sister of Tamir Rice. But as any parent who has lost a child can attest, no amount of money can ever make up for such a loss.

For days, I walked around numb. Sure, I got Canon to school and I put Theo down for his afternoon nap; somehow I even managed to put food on the table three, four, five times a day. But food I did not taste. Emotions I did not feel. The world I did not engage with, for I *could* not engage with other people. This felt too close to home. I could have been the mother who received the call that my son had been shot. My little boy, who stood in front of his class and told them that he wants to be a policeman and a farmer and maybe a space astronaut when he grows up, borrowed a toy gun from his friend and began waving it around in the park. I could see just how it happened: he began to put on a show. An audience sat around him, because some of us, like him and like me, come alive when people are watching, when we get to perform. But within seconds, the performance was over. The lights went out, in my heart and in his and in all who were affected by his unjust death. No longer would he be a policeman when he grew up, for the ones who were supposed to serve and protect us all failed to see past his large, brown body.

What if the colors had been reversed, though? What if two black or brown officers had shot a twelve-year-old white boy? Would a grand jury have worked itself to the ground to find ample evidence to indict *these* child murderers? I don't doubt the outcome of the story would have been different, but that's not the story—at least not then and not now, when we still have to have this conversation. And in a country built on values of whiteness, where the lives of white people intrinsically hold more value because they were born with skin that matches the values of the system, until the values are reversed, that *is* still the story. So we light our candles and we hold our breath and we cry our tears when we realize the severity of our actions: that we have not valued black and brown lives as much as we've valued white lives in America today.

As a mother, I not only see my children as good but also *know* they are good. I call them good, for this goodness is the essence of who they are as humans and as the beloved of God. But not everyone sees this goodness in my sons, for this goodness is not as pervasive as the Pollyanna in me so desperately wants to believe. And when this goodness is not seen, then conversations can begin in different circles. There are the conversations about submitting to a police officer, not because he or she is your friend but because he or she is *not* your friend. There are conversations about not wearing your hoodie over your head, as warmth and comfort would dictate, but keeping the fabric snug around your shoulders so as not to arouse suspicion. And there are conversations about the importance of acting outside of your culture in order to adapt to the problems that the majority culture has to face.

But maybe it's not a matter of limiting the conversation to a particular people or expanding the conversation to people like me. Instead, it's a matter of mothers and fathers everywhere, of flesh and blood, of adoption and circumstance, embracing each and every one of our children. It's a matter of raising our voices in unison and singing songs of *imago Dei* over all of our children. It's a matter of believing their goodness is universal.

I sat at my kitchen table one afternoon, staring into the Skype screen, fingers flying across the keyboard. A mutual friend had suggested I talk to Adrienne Davis, who was at the time a diversity coordinator at a private school in Durham, North Carolina.[4]

"You know, Cara," she said, "entering into this conversation and into this process is a lifelong journey. We're not going to wake up in the morning all better."

"I hear you," I replied, nodding for her to continue.

"And I see the world's way of doing this and of trying to handle this, and to an extent I agree: I'm a proponent of equity. But without the hope of Christ, it falls on deaf ears, because this conversation requires self-motivation, and at the end of the day only one thing matters: you have to care, Cara, more about my children than your children." I gulped as Adrienne folded her hands onto the table in front of her, a table nearly three thousand miles away from my own. Her words dared me to respond. Would I ever care more about her children than my own? Could that ever actually happen in my heart? I wondered if I would ever have the eyes to see Adrienne's children, to love unconditionally as God first loved me.

*L*ong after the conversation with Adrienne, I gazed at school pictures of Canon and Theo taped on the wall above my desk. Among inspirational quotes, prayers of confession, and notes of encouragement, Canon's snarky, confident grin and scrunched-up nose boldly provoke me to do, to say, to ask. His brain is a collection of facts; he digs deep into a variety of interests: *Did you know that a stingray's eyes are on top of his body, but his mouth is on the bottom of his body? Did you know that the stingray is not very good at seeing? Did you know that the stingray is a cousin of the shark?* I did not know that, but I do now, buddy. Next to him, Theo smiles good-naturedly, somehow reaching straight through the camera lens on into my heart. Taller than most of his peers, it's like other parts of him are bigger too: his vocabulary is off the charts, his personality bolder and larger than thirty-three inches would imply. He is a natural joker, a storyteller at heart. The world is his stage, the audience his oyster.

As I thought about the playground conversation, the woman's questions showed me that she did not see my boys as normal, for normal to her was a child born with white skin. My children were outside of her image of perfection, different from the picture of a white Gerber Baby ingrained in her mind. I see this on the playground and I hear it in the aisles of Target. Sometimes I feel like its presence haunts me everywhere I go.

"Oh, is she not the epitome of the Gerber Baby?" a woman cooed over an infant girl in the car seat of another woman's cart.

"She is, she is," the proud mother replied. I remember glancing down at my cart and at my infant son nestled in the car seat of my shopping cart. Was my child any less of a Gerber Baby than hers? Not in the least, but this image of the perfect baby remains more than twenty years after the brand changed its commercials, no longer featuring one infant who *was* a white child but featuring "not one baby, but dozens of faces from all different races."[5]

So when I am asked if *they* are mine, grace isn't always my response. Instead, what I want to scream on playgrounds and in lunchrooms and in Sunday school classrooms, too, is a holy *we*, a sacred *ours,* a hallowed *us.* Because if who we are together is not rooted in the acceptance of all colors, then righteous anger bubbles up—but righteous anger is more than okay, for such anger is redemptive anger, the kind of anger that "moves you to transformation and human up-building."[6] And in this spirit of divine indignation, I flip temple tables in my head and with my mouth and sometimes with my typing fingers too. I make no room for playground apologies, at least not today.

*B*ut sometimes it takes decades to put meaning around this whole idea of *we,* to learn to care more for others' children than for my own. Two-thirds of the way through writing the first draft of this book, I took a weeklong break to go on the Ruby Woo Pilgrimage, a journey of womanhood, justice, and faith, with thirty three Christian women from around the United States. The first night, in Syracuse, New York, was lazy, an evening of laughter and respite before hopping on a bus at seven the next morning, bound first for Seneca Falls, then down to New York City, Philadelphia, Maryland, and Washington, D.C. Diverse in culture, race, and ethnicity, we boasted with our Ruby Woo lips of unity, the bold red shade complimentary to every skin tone. Over the course of five days, we listened and we learned. We tried our hardest to embrace one another's journeys of discomfort and joy, knowing each one of us would leave changed in her own way.

On Monday night, we tumbled out of the bus, bleary-eyed from a six-hour ride, eager to sit at the feet of a woman we affectionately called Mama Ruby. As I learned, Rev. Dr. Ruby Sales became a voice of the southern freedom movement when, as a seventeen-year-old, she took up membership in SNCC (Student Nonviolent Coordinating Committee), becoming active in various protests and demonstrations.[7] On one such occasion, during the march from Selma to Montgomery in 1965, she and a handful of other students were arrested and jailed for six days after they protested a whites-only store. Upon their release, she and her friends went to a nearby store to buy sodas. When a disgruntled construction worker threatened Sales and pulled out a gun, a white male Episcopal seminary student pushed her out of the way, taking a bullet for her. His subsequent death furthered the impetus of her life's work as a social activist and public theologian and, decades later, as an academic. A queer woman, an African American, and a survivor of southern hate, hers is a trusted voice for those who have been marginalized and the oppressed.[8]

When Mama Ruby opens her mouth to speak, you listen. You take notes until your hand hurts, because hers is the good kind of hurt, the kind you chew on for days, weeks, months to come.

"Fighting for justice isn't something we do for others, it's something we do for ourselves. Every movement is nitty-gritty hard work that we do to redeem ourselves,"[9] Mama Ruby said into the microphone. Like my father-in-law, she spoke with deliberation, slowly chewing over each thought before more words tumbled out of her mouth. Was this because of her age, her southernness, her wisdom? I stared at my lap, transfixed by her thoughts: "Justice isn't something we do for others, but it's something we do for ourselves." This seemed contradictory to everything I had learned and read and promoted about justice. Surely anyone could see by my skin color that racial justice wasn't for me. It was *my* people who had created, enacted, and abused hierarchies of hate. As has been said, we may not have Jim Crow laws on the books, but we still have Jim Crow hate.[10] So with all this Jim Crow hate in our country today, isn't it my responsibility to fight for the justice of others? After all, I hold an awareness of the hate, of the injustice, of the present situation, and of the problem at hand. Therefore, I carry with me a burden to do better, a burden to help others know and do better too.

But as long as I remain immune to fighting for justice within myself, I only perpetuate the problem. I buy into the lie of "us and them." I believe that it's not about me, just as it's not about white people who look like me, but it's about *them:* all those black and brown people whose lives do not hold equal value. When that happens, I miss the point—even when my intentions are good, even when I'm standing up for equality in the lives of others.

Maybe that's when it hit me, maybe for the first time in my life: if redemption is for everyone, then redemption is for me too. I knew this—redemption is at the heart of the gospel. The words of a hymn I sang as a girl flooded my mind: *I know that my Redeemer lives. What comfort this sweet sentence gives! He lives, he lives, who once was dead. He lives, my everliving Head.* I had known it. I had believed it. I had preached and taught it to others, believing that the same redemption that had changed my life could also change the lives of others.

But when it came to racial justice, I hadn't thought redemption belonged to me. When Mama Ruby told me that justice was for me too, I was reminded that I could be made brand new. I am not held hostage by the color of my skin, nor am I in trouble with my history—even if a litany of apologies and reparations and change, on behalf of both my country and me, still needs to happen. But "an impulse to freedom still lives in the hearts of broken people."[11] And I just might be the most broken of all.

So I cling to justice because this impulse toward freedom, joy, and wholeness lives within me, begging and fighting for redemption. I become a justice-slinger mostly for myself, and as a byproduct, also for the world around me. And when I make this connection, I wonder if I'm beginning to understand the beloved community. Mama Ruby's thoughts loop through my mind like a broken record:

"It's all about the mountaintop. To Dr. King, the mountaintop was not a space 'but a collective experience. You are the one who imagines and creates a beloved community. There exists a beloved community consciousness, a higher level of consciousness, where the *I* and the *we,* rather than the *us* and the *they,* learn to harmonize with one another.'"[12]

Together we sit, every single one of us in need of redemption, every man, woman, and child invited to partake of the table of grace. As a beloved people, we draw water from the well. We dine with the Lamb. This banquet table extends across fields and mountains and oceans too, and at each seat, the *I* is not negated but celebrated in all its particularities. Here, we honor the *imago Dei,* for in this place we celebrate our beloved identity as children of God.

I closed my eyes at mere thought of it all: how I wanted this mountaintop of a place, this collective where we all sit side by side at the great table in harmony. I wanted this for my boys, and I wanted this for the woman on the playground. I wanted it for my friends Julie and Adrienne and for their families, and I wanted it for the family who ached for their lost son, Tamir. I wanted it for every Gerber Baby everywhere and for the women I journeyed alongside on the pilgrimage. Not stingy with my invitation, I wanted this beloved community to extend table to table around the world, ten thousand times over. Between bites of redemption, we would sip of the cup of justice. And even if it took a lifetime to understand, we would come to find the meaning of *us* not in the *I* but in the *we,* not in the *theirs* but in the *ours* of one who is loved.

CHAPTER 16

Lamentations

It happened again last night, as it has nearly every night for the last three years: chronic back pain jolted me awake in the middle of the night. Having tasted sleep, I was even more desperate for a remedy to the pain. But then a doctor listened to me and sent me to a specialist, who in a stark and sterile room whispered the words *arthritis of the spine*. Diagnosis thought to be confirmed, I heeded the specialist's advice and began downing the prescribed horse pills three times a day.

James happened to be out of town on a work trip. By the end of the second day of taking the pills, my body rebelled against me: hives sprouted up and down my chest, trailing like ivy across my shoulders and up to my neck, down my stomach and onto my legs. My body afire, I ran around the house in nothing but a sports bra and running shorts, the touch of fabric torturous to my skin. My eyelids drooped, threatening to swell shut if I didn't do something, anything, right away, even if it meant leaving the house after the dinner hour by myself with both of my boys.

Now, as any parent of young children can attest, something called the witching hour descends on households all across America between five and seven o'clock every evening. Although pint-sized humans are tired and ready to sleep, they don't know how to use their words to advocate for their needs. They don't know how to say, "Hey, Mama! I'm tired, and I should really start my wind-down time so I can wake up bright-eyed and bushy-tailed tomorrow morning." They don't do that, not in the least. Instead, they go feral. They run circles around the house. They attempt dangerous jumping feats off the couch. They boss Alexa around, commanding her to, "PLEASE PLAY THE BEST HOLIDAY DANCE MUSIC EVER, NOW!" when it's the middle of March, and really, they should be snug in their beds counting sheep, snoring soundly.

It was in this state of wildness that Canon, Theo, and I put on our bravest faces and drove a quarter-mile down the road to the grocery store. Everyone else in town seemed to be at the prescription counter that night as my fully clothed body itched and I tried to get the boys to sit crisscross applesauce on the floor. Past the point of no return, as the pharmacist rattled off a list of directives for my steroid pills, the boys began to play Ring Around the Rosie around a display sign. That's when *she* stepped out of line.

"Don't you know this is a store? Don't you know you're supposed to be quiet, that you're not allowed to act this way, that you shouldn't be running around a grocery store in the first place?" As her shouting continued, everything within me went silent, gunned down by her outburst. Rendered mute, I couldn't utter a word in response. Meanwhile, the boys stared at her, wondering if they should smile, if they should say hello. The pharmacist stared at her. I stared at her. Every patron standing in line and pushing a cart around the aisles of Safeway stared at her, aghast.

Even if a two-year-old and a four-year-old are acting like a primitive pack of hyenas, you don't yell at the children. You yell at Twitter. You yell in CAPS LOCK to everyone on your social media platforms. But you don't yell at the babies.

I picked my jaw up off the ground, wiping tears from my eyes. Grabbing their hands, we began the slow march away from her and from the scene of the hurt. The perfect words of retaliation would come to me in an hour or two, but for now, we just had to get out of there.

"Have a nice day!" I shouted over my shoulder, a bit of snark mingling with my tears. But she wasn't done with us yet.

"Just a reminder, you're getting a tax break for those things!" Aghast, I stood there as tears rolled down my face. The boys stood silently beside me while the adults nearby stood mute to the spectacle, mouths hung open.

"Lady, I'm doing the best I can," I replied and looked at the kindhearted, Cheerios-loving, *Curious George*-obsessed, snuggly, doe-eyed sons I love more than life itself. I thought about who they are. I thought about how the way I see them isn't always the way the rest of the world sees them. I know the iceberg of humanity that lives beneath the surface, an iceberg of feeling and personality, of likes and dislikes, of brilliant, spongey minds who want to learn and do good and please their mama and daddy, of children of God who are loved simply because God loved them first.

"It sounds like you just encountered your first taste of racism," my friend Rene said to me a couple of days later. As I am often prone to do, I had begun to laugh about the encounter, blown away by a stranger's audacity toward my children and toward me. The laughter was mine alone, though. I shook my head vehemently, not wanting to believe that someone would judge my babies by the color of their skin, not wanting to admit that someone would believe her white body to be better than their brown bodies. But when we make people the "other," the social norms are not the same. As Rene reminded me, in American culture, we don't often see black boys as boys but we see them as men. The expectations become different for them, because these young boys don't get to be children. They become things and tax write-offs instead of two- and four-year-old boys who fancy a game in a grocery store. For Rene, a biracial woman who identifies as black, there wasn't a question in her mind that I had tasted the bitterness of racism.

The smile on my face waned. It was no longer a laughing matter.

*N*early a year later, my friend Shannon and I wove our way through the National African American Museum of History and Culture in Washington, D.C. Two days before, we'd sat at the feet of Mama Ruby, and now, on our last full day of the pilgrimage, our bodies ached with a wild kind of exhaustion. Desperate to return home, I longed for enough time to filter all of the information I'd internalized that week. Shannon longed for respite too, but hers included a recess from the pain of her body. Still recovering from double knee surgery, her legs screamed in agony. Occasionally, she walked without assistance, but sometimes she needed her walking sticks, and sometimes her wheelchair. That day in the museum, her body begged for the comfort of her chair.

We were mostly silent as we wheeled through the museum, and an elevator took us to the basement, into the hulls of slave ships that transported millions of Africans from their home countries to Europe, the Americas, and beyond. We made our way through darkened, narrow passages designed to resemble the cramped living conditions of the ships. Our minds and bodies were transported to our country's beginnings, to the 1400s, when slavery around the world was a temporary status not based on a person's outward appearance. With each sideward glance, the wheels of Shannon's chair clicked in rotation, just as the years ticked upward too. We traveled through the 1600s and into the late 1700s, the murals and quotes and wax depictions of each scene an aching remembrance of injustice. But when we got to 1776, we stopped and stared at an irony of massive, bolded words slapped onto the wall daring us to disagree.

> All men are created equal . . .
> With certain unalienable rights . . .
> Whenever any form of government
> Becomes destructive of these ends,
> It is the right of the people to alter
> Or to abolish it.[1]

The gilded letters of the Declaration of Independence rose above the atrocities of injustice, its message the greatest paradox of liberty.[2] Sure, the statement was true for those of us born with white skin, but it wasn't true for everyone. By the American Revolution, slavery was an institution, a racial caste associated with African ancestry. America was a country built on the backs of slave labor and upon land stolen from the native population. Then, in 1787, the government mandated that a black person be counted as only three-fifths of a white person for purposes of determining representation in Congress.[3] Black people were held to be less human than white people. In the eyes of the government, African Americans had *not* been created equal, nor did they possess certain unalienable rights, and now, nearly two hundred and fifty years later, this inequality still exists. We continue to cling to hope for millions of black and brown Americans still treated like chattel by systems of injustice, for those yet to possess equal dignity in the eyes of the government and their fellow countrymen.

For too long I refused to let myself see history's one-sided affair, listening to and learning from the stories of my past, stories told from the point of view of the oppressors. But now, I didn't know where I fit in. I'd begun to examine history through another lens. Images of

James and Canon and Theo flashed through my mind, their faces a reminder of the reality of hardship.

Shannon and I journeyed upward, ascending wide ramps to the eighteenth and nineteenth centuries. Every inch of the museum told the stories I had not always cared to hear, provided quotes I had not always taken the time to read. By the time we reached the early 1860s and stood before Lincoln's Emancipation Proclamation, I yearned for hope, desperate for a sliver of optimism in a decree I'd long thought ended slavery once and for all. But as Shannon and I looped around the next corner, we came face to face with the Jim Crow laws, with our country's hideous legacy of lynching, with the atrocities of sharecropping. By the time we reached the midtwentieth century, I wanted to run to a dark corner and hide, crouching like a small child trying to escape, like a little girl who doesn't want to be seen. I didn't want to be a white woman in that space, because I didn't want to carry the injustice—the injustice that was mine—on my shoulders any longer. I wanted a thousand absolutions to release me from the pain, to free my lungs of the sobs welling up inside.

But as the hours ticked by, I knew this pain was mine to hold. No longer did I have the right to walk away or to distance myself from the atrocities. I was bound both to the stories of the oppressed and to the oppressor, to histories I couldn't rewrite and to futures I desperately hoped to change.

Then, rounding a corner into the early 1950s, we entered the private exhibit of Emmett Till, a place where cameras, recording devices, and cell phones are prohibited.

"He was the first, but he won't be the last," the guard whispered to a woman as she entered the darkened room. The man shook his head before offering her a half smile, his words a deep kind of knowing, I suppose. On August 24, 1955, after spending the summer with his cousins in Money, Mississippi, fourteen-year-old Emmett Till went to a country store with a group of his friends and family. Accounts of the incident vary: some say he bragged about having a white girlfriend back home, so his buddies dared him to prove it. Others say he whistled at Carolyn Bryant, the white woman behind the counter, and said, "Bye, baby," as he walked out of her store. Whatever happened that day, the young teenager ignored his mother's warnings to take care because of his race. Four days later, Bryant's husband, Roy, and his half brother, J. W. Milam, "made Emmett carry a 75-pound cotton-gin fan to the bank of the Tallahatchie River and ordered him to take off his clothes. The two men then beat him nearly to death, gouged out his eye, shot him in the head, and then threw his body, tied to the cotton-gin fan with barbed wire, into the river."[4] A week after the incident in the country store, authorities found Till's body at the bottom of a nearby river. His face was so disfigured from the beating and his body was so swollen that his uncle could identify Emmett only by the initialed ring he wore on his finger.

While the details of the boy's murder are gruesome, his death changed the world. Emmett's mother, Mamie Till-Mobley, ordered his body to be sent back to Chicago, his hometown, despite protests from local authorities who hoped to—literally—bury the story in the ground. But she would not back down.

"I wanted the world to see what they did to my baby," Mamie cried,[5] choosing to expose his body in an open casket funeral to the thousands who would view his remains in person and to the hundreds of thousands who would see a photograph of a mother looking at her son's ravaged body in *Jet* magazine. "That must have been at that time the largest single civil rights demonstration in American history," Jesse Jackson said at the time of her death in 2003.[6] Through one woman's determination, the American public could no longer pretend to ignore the evidence of hate before them, so much so that many historians believe that her single act of bravery inspired Rosa

Parks not to give up her seat on the bus, leading to the beginning of the civil rights movement.[7]

While Mamie's strength prompted others to action, there was no justice for Emmett Till. Two weeks after his body was buried, Roy and J. W. went to trial in a segregated courthouse in Sumner, Mississippi. After sixty-seven minutes of deliberation, an all-white jury found the men not guilty of all charges, citing that the state failed to prove the identity of the body. Charges of kidnapping were never filed, and when *Time* magazine interviewed the pair a couple of months later, they admitted to murdering Till. Protected by double jeopardy, it was too late for a conviction.

But Mamie Till-Mobley wasn't close to being done yet. "I want y'all to stand by me because it's going to be a fight, and if you will stand by me, I will stand by you, because I am not afraid,"[8] she said upon deciding to showcase her dead son's body. As I stood in the museum that day, her grief became my grief. His death became my death. Was Emmett Till all that different from my boys, from all of our boys? Would I have reacted the same? Would I have chosen to fight, to speak out against hate, to keep putting one foot in front of the other even though a part of me had died? My lungs constricted, as a final heat of sorrow rose up in my chest and tears streamed down my face. I wasn't shy of being seen. Every part of me seemed to cry out in pain, broken by the loss of an innocent boy, broken by the strength of a woman who kept fighting even as she lost a piece of her heart. Broken by the lack of justice then, now, and maybe always, a lack of justice that made me wonder why we still had to fight for racial justice and equality when there shouldn't have been a need for a conversation about racial justice and equality in the first place.

But even in my brokenness, I knew the fight was hardly over. "Mamie," I whispered, "I stand by you. Help me not to be afraid, because sometimes this fight overwhelms me." I knew it in my gut, but that day the truth made its way into my heart: standing up for justice means speaking even if my voice trembles. It means typing words that make others angry and uncomfortable, sentences and paragraphs and chapters that cost me friendships, that might even take a toll on James and the boys.

After staring one last time at her picture, I walked back to Shannon's chair. "I'm ready," I said, before whispering it again. Not only was I ready to leave the room, but I was ready to do whatever it took to stand alongside Mamie Till.

A month later, Shannon and I traded text messages, piecing together our experiences of the pilgrimage and of the contrasts between she who sat and she who stood. Shannon, a white woman, is the mother of six biological and adopted children, her heart a perfect blend of sass and holiness, her words a sounding board for truth. Without a doubt, she is unafraid to proclaim a gospel of verity from the mountaintops. Like me, she tries her hardest to leverage her privilege to give voice and face to the marginalized.

In the museum that day, we wore matching T-shirts that said, "We are our foremothers' wildest dreams," but I wondered whether that was actually true for either of us. She was probably more like the worst nightmare of her ancestors, who owned and operated a southern plantation. Her parents grew up with a normalized view of segregation. They didn't fight against it. A year before our trip, she wrote, "I haven't been to the museum yet, but I expect there are exhibits on slavery. My ancestors include white slave owners in the South. That's my history too."[9] As I wheeled Shannon through the museum that day, she examined everything through a lens not of the present but of the past, of the oppressors who rallied against the freedom and rights of African Americans. Meanwhile, I was a nightmare of a different sort: I saw the exhibits through the eyes of my husband and my children's ancestry, of the oppressed who fought for freedom and for the rights they deserved. I looked for an escape from the pain, for a way to hide from my skin. There, I found refuge in the oneness I felt with the mother of a slain boy.

Looking back, I believe Shannon and I were doing the best we could. But neither one of us realized there might be a better way, a middle road for us on our journey.

We had to learn how to hold the oppressor and honor the oppressed, for love can redeem everything, including both the oppressor and the oppressed. We had to enter the fullness of lament.

I don't always readily enter lament. I often want a happy, hopeful version of Jesus, a personal savior to call my own. I want to skip entire portions of the church calendar, ignoring the dreariness of Lent and of Advent so I can get straight to the hope and glory of Easter. It's as if I stand in my son's preschool classroom and point to the poster of cartoon faces on the wall. Although it illustrates thirty different feelings—hysteria, sadness, anger, confusion, lovestrickenness, and boredom, among others—I often want to permanently reside in the land of happiness. I want a quick fix for my experiences of racial brokenness.[10] I want to slap a bandaid on the problem of pain, especially if I feel shame, especially if the burden of guilt lies on people who look like me. But this is no way to live, for this is no way to heal, nor is it any way to grow.

We were not made to experience only a single emotion. We were created to experience a myriad of feelings, including deep pain. So we are also to be people of lament, to voice holy complaints and protests and griefs aloud, to enter the brokenness of injustice and pain.

Lament teaches me to shed light on stories of sorrow, to dig up the burdens of oppression for both the oppressor and the oppressed. When tragedy strikes, I no longer ignore suffering and death in the world around me but I take notice. I pay attention to the hate, noticing the ways history has often been painted by a white point of view. But I don't stop there. I take action. I enter the sorrow of injustice, mourning with those who mourn, weeping with those who weep.[11] I breathe in the wounds of the unknown among me, of the immigrants and refugees and asylum seekers in my midst, of the black and brown brothers and sisters in my neighborhood and in my city whose injuries I have not cared for. I sit with the pain I have inflicted on others. I mourn the pain others have inflicted on me.

Then, because I have no other choice, I become a person marked by holy sorrow, not as an individual but as a part of the greater whole. Righteous wails fill the air as every voice, including those I have not given power to and those I have ignored, march in a funeral dirge. The boundless rules of lament become my only response.[12]

No longer do we ignore the suffering and pain and death of others, but with compassion as our only sword, we listen and we enter in to heartache. We don't bind ourselves with apathy, but we pay attention to the past and we drink of the present, eyes opened wide toward the future. Then, balancing on a scale of hope and lament, we cry out for justice and for peace, for ourselves and for the world around us. These are our fellow human beings, after all.

That day in the museum, though, no part of me wanted to participate in or pass on a legacy of hate not to my children, my husband, my brothers and sisters of color. But walking forward means embracing every part of my story, including the parts I want to forget and the parts I want to be absolved of responsibility. It means stepping into places of sorrow, letting the tears fall, dressing in uniforms of lament.

I think of my grandmother. Once, standing in the living room of her home, she watched as a black man on television began beating his wife. "Meggie," she said to my cousin, who was there visiting, "please don't ever marry a black man. He'll beat you!" She whistled away, without a care in the world, while young Meghan looked back at her, startled by her outburst. The family blamed it on Alzheimer's, on a mind not fully intact, on a brain not alive to the reality of the world. She died long before James came into my life, but I sometimes wonder what she would have said to me had her mind still been there, had the disease not been an excuse for her words. And I think of my grandfather, who, upon meeting James for the first time in his nursing home, yelled, "Darkie!" James and I looked at one another. *Did he really just say what I think he said?* It was a greeting we tried to forget; dementia had staked claim to his mind too. Though he had been a brilliant theologian and pastor for more than five decades, all the accolades in heaven couldn't protect his mouth from the racist words of his youth. A thousand more stories come to mind, stories of the living and the dead, stories of my ancestors that shaped my earliest thoughts, stories that make me realize how a lineage of inequality lives in my bones too.

In love and in pain, I embrace the stereotypes buried within me. Their stories I am, and my stories they are, for ours is a story of embracing, of repenting, and of becoming. Entering the beautiful and ugly parts of my past, I do the only thing I can do: I lament. I let myself sit with the pain and feel the weight of injustice, doing this with the living and the dead and with all the saints who walk through sorrow's doors. We say I'm sorry. We ask for forgiveness. We make our amends. We sit in silence and let ourselves feel the weight of sorrow.

Then, sprinkling ourselves with a generous dusting of grace, we nod toward all the future saints: to my sons and to their cousins, to all those little ones born with fire in their bones. We honor them with a legacy of truth. And with tears in our eyes, we find a middle road, choosing to tell every side of the story.

CHAPTER 17

Tramp, Tramp, Tramping of Feet

"So are you an activist?" a new friend asked me one morning over coffee. Three out of our four children played together in the basement while her baby sat comfortably in the high chair, absorbed in smashing bite sized pieces of banana everywhere but in his mouth.

"Me? An activist? I guess. But it doesn't always seem that way. At what point do you become an activist? When you give yourself the label, when you take a class, when you march at a rally? Or is it when others call you an activist?" I shrugged and wondered whether activism could live in the daily grind of motherhood, in the midst of wiping bottoms, making peanut butter and jelly sandwiches, and building Lego towers. As the boys got older, I began to spend more time with my words, leaning into the part of me that called herself a writer. I read more books and listened to more podcasts and had more conversations about race and faith and justice. And just as opinions about injustice began to grow in me, I realized my privilege in not having to say anything in the fight for equality in the first place. I realized my privilege in being able to choose which battles I engaged in, because having a choice was the very definition of privilege. After a couple of years, I used my voice to speak out more—on various social media platforms, from the pulpit, and in online and print articles. But still, I hardly called myself an activist. I was more like an activist in training, or an activist with part-time leanings, whenever the confines of motherhood permitted activism.

But then, on a cold Monday morning in January, the four of us set out to march. James and I bundled the boys up in their warmest winter coats, stuffing scarves and hats and gloves into his backpack, along with enough snacks to feed our troop for a week. Really, we didn't know if participating in Seattle's MLK March was the best idea we'd ever had as parents, or if it would quickly make the short list of Things to Never Do with Your Children, but we were desperate. Less than two months before, our family moved two states north, from Oakland, California, to Seattle, Washington, for a job for James. We said farewell to the city we thought we'd settle down in, to a neighborhood and a people that had stolen our hearts. Like a baby bird tapping its beak against the outer shell, we soon found ourselves tapping against the hard outer shells of transition. We would do whatever it took to break free from the heartache of moving, from the confines of starting over. And maybe it would all start with the tramp, tramp, tramp of marching feet, with putting one foot in front of the other, next to each other and alongside strangers whose hearts were bent toward justice too. James and the boys and I would march beside thousands of other people, each stomping foot a declaration of anger and sadness and hope, each voice an invitation to join the rallying cry.

We would go as far as the boys could walk. We would hold a construction-paper sign colored in by the resident four-year-old. "Canon, what do you want the poster to read?" I asked him the afternoon before, reminding him that it could say something about Dr. King, whom he'd been learning about in his preschool class.

"Dr. King loved everybody, like Jesus!" he replied, and his words became the day's declaration of truth, the phrase we would shout as we walked along the parade route, if the crowd fell silent.

But the morning of the march, Canon somehow got sand in his eye. By the time we found a parking spot in southeast Seattle, loaded up the stroller, and began trotting to the parade route, he writhed in pain, squeezing his eyes shut and grabbing at his face. Theo sat on top of James' shoulders, taking it all in, clutching the top of his father's smooth bald head for security. I pushed Canon in the stroller and, momentarily losing all sense of compassion, wondered if my son was just faking it, if he merely wanted to find his way to a playground instead. Taking our place near the end of the parade we began to march, but within a block or two, his cries prompted us to pull over and check on him, again, to flush his eye out with water, again. *March, stop. March, stop. March, stop.* Finally, after we had marched and stopped too many times and probably hadn't made it a half mile, his cries hadn't abated. Our homemade sign still tucked in the bottom of the stroller, we flagged down a paramedic for help.

"It's okay," the paramedic said, maybe to Canon, maybe to us "It happens." Handing our boy a bag of saline solution, he pointed ahead, the last of the marchers a football field length in front of us. Our marching days were over, at least for the time being. But that wouldn't stop my family from living into the legacy set before us, from teaching others and reminding ourselves to love everybody, just like Dr. King and just like Jesus. Maybe we were activists after all.

I tend to believe that marching courses through our veins, or at least through the veins of James and the boys, and then vicariously to me. Although my grandparents, cofounders of the Jews for Jesus movement in the early seventies, passed out tracts on the streets of San Francisco with the organization, my heritage isn't marked by stomping feet. We were the teachers and the police officers, the preachers and the school administrators, the helpers of the professional world, but not the ones who stood on the frontlines shouting for change. But in 1966, my father-in-law organized the Meredith March Against Fear, a march that would come to be known as the last great walk of the civil rights movement, as well as the beginning of the Black Power movement.

Of course, this wasn't his intention for the march. Although three years had passed since James Meredith became the first African American to graduate from the University of Mississippi, an obvious need to stand up for the civil rights of every citizen remained. Within weeks of my father-in-law's graduation, Martin Luther King Jr. solidified his standing as a national figure, leading hundreds of thousands in the historic March on Washington, ending with the famous "I Have a Dream" speech. Two years later, King and other nonviolent leaders led a five-day walk from Selma to Montgomery, a march that not only resulted in voting rights for black Alabamans but also birthed the Voting Rights Act of 1965. Within a year, though, activity within the movement slowed, a trend that continued until King's death in 1968, the year that also marked the movement's official end.

But the need for equality hadn't lessened. Following graduation, my father-in-law stood on the sidelines, pursuing more education, not always associating himself with the greater cause. Although he had been marked as a figurehead of the movement, it was a label slapped on him by others. And were James Meredith sitting beside you today, he'd be the first to tell you that he does what he wants. He does not conform to classifications but conforms to his own destiny and to the duties of divine responsibility. According to author and historian Ann Bausum, "he wanted to battle something even bigger than Ole Miss, something even bigger than segregation. This time he wanted to battle fear, the fear that pulsed through so many racial interactions in the South."[1] The fear that lived in the hearts of his fellow black Mississippians made him set his sights on a 220-mile walk from Memphis, Tennessee, to Jackson, Mississippi. If he could just walk, if he could just keep putting one foot in front of the other, then his steps might further encourage black voter participation—and secure their future vote, were he ever to run for office. So he prepared to walk without fanfare, without military intervention and police protection, and without thousands walking beside him. Unlike King and other protest organizers who followed with an equal kind of courage but with a Gandhian model of protest, my father-in-law "embraced the era's more traditional view of manhood, believing that men proved their worth with courageous behavior."[2] James Meredith disliked the movement's inclusion of women and children, and on the afternoon of June 5, 1966, with a handful of followers and $11.35 in his pockets, my father-in-law started walking. He didn't know where he would sleep or how he would eat, but he believed the good Negroes of Mississippi would take care of him.

But then there was an enemy. On the second day of his walk, a white man from Tennessee, Aubrey James Norvell, ambushed him, shooting four hundred and fifty shotgun pellets at him. Although James Meredith wanted to walk alone, without protection, law enforcement officers, journalists, and other witnesses stood nearby and, after the shock of the surprise attack, came to his aid and arrested Norvell on the spot.[3]

Years later, when James and I were newlyweds, some of the high school students I worked with in ministry invited the two of us to speak to their history classes about James' father. We debated it: even though my husband wasn't shy about the merits of his dad's fame, he hadn't made it his goal to publicly tout his standing as the son of James Meredith. This was a big deal, we admitted, but it was a big deal we could do together. That morning, the rhythms of each US history class looked similar: my husband talked, the students listened. Much to everyone's chagrin, I added a couple of quippy comments, believing I *knew* the story since I had been a part of the family for two whole years by that point, but of course, the students asked more questions of James. He was the main attraction. As the day went on, I drank of their obvious admiration for him. But at the end of each forty-five-minute period, I pulled an old teacher's trick out of my hat. Desirous to empower the students to *see,* I asked them to put words to a stack of photographs we'd brought along with us.

"What do you notice about these pictures?" I asked as thirty enlarged images were passed around the room, all of different events in James Meredith's life: A picture of thousands of military officers standing in silent formation at The Grove. A photograph of him sitting in a classroom by himself, every desk around him empty as the professor lectured from the front. (The majority of the white students left the room when he entered.) A picture of him perched in front of numerous microphone stands while his twin boys, James and Joseph, climbed on top of him, clamoring for their daddy's attention. Then, an image the students didn't quite know how to interpret: a photograph of him lying on the ground, writhing in pain, blood seeping into the ground.

"He's all alone."

"Why isn't anyone helping him?"

"A photographer was able to snap a picture but wasn't able to see if he was okay first? What's up with that?"

The sixteen- and seventeen-year-olds with us that morning nailed it, as teenagers often do. (The photographer, Jack Thornell, won the 1967 Pulitzer Prize for photography, although after snapping the picture he reportedly "drove back to Memphis in a panic, convinced he would be fired for failing to photograph both the assailant and the victim."[4] His fear lay not over his inability to help but over his failure to capture the proper images.)

After my father-in-law was shot, he began yelling a string of commands to those who numbly stood by watching:

"Isn't anyone going to help me?"

"Get a car and get me in it!"[5]

Within minutes, an ambulance arrived and transported him to a Memphis hospital, where doctors declared that his wounds were not life threatening. Later, when a journalist inquired about his condition, the doctor-in-training replied, "'If he had been an ordinary n— on an ordinary Saturday night,' . . . 'we'd have swabbed his ass with merthiolate [an antiseptic] and sent him home.'"[6] But as had already been proven, he was no ordinary man.

Then, a silver lining, a ray of hope inserted into a tale of attempted murder. Within hours of the shooting, leaders from five leading civil-rights organizations came to his aid. The "Big Five," which included Martin Luther King Jr. of the SCLC (Southern Christian Leadership Conference) and Stokely Carmichael of SNCC (Student Nonviolent Coordinating Committee), as well as leaders of three other organizations,[7] converged at his bedside. In a way, it's a modern-day retelling of the parable of the good Samaritan: In a story that starts with a bloodied, side-of-the-road pain, a priest sees the man lying on the side of the road but does not help him. He crosses to the other side and snaps a Pulitzer Prize–winning picture. Another religious man, a Levite, sees the man in pain but averts his gaze. His focus on righteous heavenly realms, he walks right past the hurting man. Maybe, if the man is lucky, the Levite throws a bottle of antiseptic across the road toward the body—after all, he took an oath to treat his patients well, even if he believes the color of their skin warrants them to be less than him. But then, a Samaritan, or as luck would have it in this retelling of the story, five Samaritans come to the aid of a man who hadn't asked for any association with them in the first place. "But a Samaritan, as he traveled, came where the man was; and when he saw him, he took pity on him. He went to him and bandaged his wounds, pouring on oil and wine. Then he put the man on his own donkey, brought him to an inn and took care of him. The next day he took out two denarii and gave them to the innkeeper. 'Look after him,' he said, 'and when I return, I will reimburse you for any extra expense you may have.'"[8]

The ones who had mercy on James Meredith bandaged his wounds by committing to finish the walk for him. They took care of him the only way they knew how, by transforming one man's walk into a protest march with upwards of fifteen thousand men, women, and children by the time it reached Jackson. For nearly twenty days, they marched, stomping feet against violence and against racial fears, rallying their cries in support of voter registration and equality for all Americans.[9] And at the end, the march did exactly what its originator had intended: it helped alleviate fear, prompting several thousand African Americans to register to vote, all because five Good Samaritans came to the rescue of one wounded man.

"There is nothing more powerful to dramatize an injustice like the tramp, tramp, tramp of marching feet,"[10] King said in a speech on the first day he and the others joined the march. He, for one, hadn't realized the full significance of the event. Not only would this mark the end of the civil rights movement, but also it would mark the beginning of the Black Power movement. As King continued to cry out for freedom, Stokely Carmichael shook the movement to its core, calling instead for black power. No longer did the rallying cry sound like this:

What do you want? FREEDOM!
When do you want it? NOW!

What do you want? FREEDOM!
When do you want it? NOW![11]

But according to historians, the cry sounded more like this:

What do you want? BLACK POWER!
What do you want? BLACK POWER!
What do you want? BLACK POWER!
What do you want? BLACK POWER![12]

Race riots broke out across the country, and the media blamed the changing bent of the movement for it, including violence the marchers faced from Mississippian white supremacists. But Carmichael was marching for something more than mere liberty, something that would get his people somewhere: although King had laid the groundwork for equality, the nonviolent philosophies of the movement could take African Americans only so far. "To him, integration in a white-dominated America meant assimilation by default," with an ultimate decision to "move the organization away from a philosophy of pacifism and escalate the group's militancy to emphasize armed self-defense, black business ownership and community control,"[13] writes Jamil Smith in an article for *Time* magazine. The need for self-determination on behalf of African Americans was great, the movement "a vision of black grandeur and, indeed, power in a trying time, when more than 41 percent of African Americans were at or below the poverty line and comprised nearly a third of the nation's poor."[14] Just as the civil rights movement came to a close, a different rallying cry began against racial oppression, this one celebrating blackness at its core.

Meanwhile, James Meredith rejoined the march for the last couple of days, as his body allowed, but he stayed mute, especially on the question of violence. He was, after all, a military man through and through, and sometimes believed that violent solutions were necessary, whether or not such words ever came out of his mouth. Years later, he wondered whether the phrase black power was really all that different from the protest anthem "We Shall Overcome,"[15] just as he had wondered whether he ever received full citizenship not as a black man but as a human.

As for me, I didn't live through it and I wasn't there, but one thing proved itself true: nothing was ever the same, not for those present that night and not for those halfway across the country. And that, I'd say, is a very good thing.

*M*y mind wandered back to my solo trip to Mississippi, to a question my father-in-law kept asking that I never seemed to answer correctly, not for him, nor for myself.

Driving down potholed roads in downtown Jackson, he asked, "Why are you writing this book?"

"Because people are fascinated about a journey of a white woman who married your son," I replied.

He shook his head.

Standing on black pavement in the parking lot of Tougaloo College, he asked, "Why are you writing this book?"

"Because I have a story to tell," I said. "Because white people need to understand that issues of race have something to do with them. Because stories of interracial marriage and biracial children are few and far between."

He shook his fists in the air, frustrated by my response.

As I pushed him in a wheelchair through the Mississippi State Capitol, he asked, "Why are you writing this book?"

"Because I want justice for my black and brown brothers and

sisters," I said, exasperated. I wanted to crack the code. The little girl within me, the one who stood shyly in the corner with pigtails and ribbons in her hair, desperately wanted to say the right thing to him. After all, he is my second father. But I couldn't give him the answer he wanted to hear, at least not then.

"I'm not doing this for you, you know," he said to me on our last afternoon, referring to our time together. He had dropped everything in his schedule to be with me, to answer my questions, to do and speak as I pleased.

"I know."

"I'm doing this for those boys," he replied.

I nodded, understanding that the gift of the previous days with him was for them. But the book that I was writing and the answer he wanted me to utter? That had to do entirely with me.

As a white woman, I can often believe that fighting for justice means standing alongside my brothers and sisters of color, working together to bring about change. I fight for racial justice because systemic racism toward black and brown lives still exists. I cry out against the chains of oppression because although we are equal in our status as human beings, we have not all been found equal in the eyes of society and in the eyes of each other. I believe we are all called children of God, but I know that in the face of racist rhetoric, I have not always come to the aid of those who have been broken and bloodied and left by the side of the road. I have not always heeded the call to be a good neighbor. Knowing this, I fight, I rally, I call myself an activist, even if it sometimes feels like I'm still trying on the phrase. But I keep fighting, channeling the voices of Mamie Till-Mobley, Martin Luther King Jr., and my father-in-law too. I walk in the holy paths of my grandparents before evil took their minds, and I love in the way my parents loved me, even if ours is sometimes a road paved with apologies and lessons yet to learn. With each step,

I cling to one thought: although the moral arc of the universe is long, it does ultimately bend toward justice.[16] Then, like millions before me, I march. I put one foot in front of the other, believing that the tramp, tramp, tramp of my marching feet powerfully dramatizes the effects of injustice.

My marching is not for my children, though, nor is it for my husband, nor is it for my brothers and sisters of color, even though they are more than worthy of my marching, their lives more than marked by dignity. I march for myself, stomping my feet for a justice and a wholeness and a peace that are also mine. Because when I allow redemption to take hold of me, a funny thing happens: I can't help but want this redemption for others too. I gulp down the justice offered me and I extend it to everyone I meet, for there is flourishing when wholeness takes root in our bones.

Here, the journey comes full circle.[17] I don't want to keep it for myself, but I want to sprinkle the sidewalks with fistfuls of redemptive confetti, my steps marked by a splendor of color. Here, I want to see those who've been silenced and oppressed not merely be given a seat at the table but handed the microphone so we can glory in the amplification of every voice. Here, whitened walls of injustice come tumbling down, one honest and gritty story at a time. And here, I finally find an answer to my father-in-law's question. I tell him about sitting at the feet of Mama Ruby one night and of realizing that fighting for justice isn't something we do for others, but it's something we do for ourselves. Then I start marching all over again, begging righteousness to dwell deeply in my soul, asking goodness to reign over my heart.

Justice is for all of us. Or so I'm beginning to believe.

Afterword by James Henry Meredith

What is love? It has been said that true love is colorblind, which is another way of saying that the color of someone's skin should have no meaningful influence on how one treats a neighbor as oneself. They say there's an absence of boundaries as we deal relationally with other people, but the cultural, social, racial, and economic differences people have used to create divisions and boundaries, particularly to true love, are present. And for true love to really be true, you have to cross the boundaries others have put in place.

But true love also ignores the foolishness of saying a person shouldn't date someone because they're a different race. When I think about this foolishness, I think about how true right is a taste of heaven, the kingdom of God touching earth, ignoring what our human eyes see when we want to live in a land of social constructs.

What a gift, then, both to see the particularities of who we are on the outside and the inside and to live in a world that crosses boundaries of body, mind, and soul. Perhaps like my father and like countless others who have gone before me, I get to experience love in a different dimension, like I'm looking through a kaleidoscope. Here I see an ocean of fingerprints, all made in the image of God—a colorful, perfect tapestry of life. In this world, there is a variety of color, a life of color, a celebration of color.

I don't mean to sound trite, but it is a blessing to be married to Cara, to be on this journey of life with her, our boys, and this divine circle of family and friends. Just as I gave her permission to share parts of my story, I give you permission to enter into the stories of your life and your people too. Although I cannot speak for my wife, my hope is that our story puts a dent in the story of your life. Whether it invites you to lament, to rejoice, to accept your redemption, or to fight against systems of injustice for the very first time, we walk this journey with you.

—James Henry Meredith, June 18, 2018

Acknowledgments

*I*t takes a village to write a book, or so I've been told. Even though I think I should push against the gender gap and *not* thank those who've come alongside us to hang out with the boys so I could get my chapters in, I'm so grateful for everyone who did. To Gadisa, Fernanda, Ben's dad (that's you, Josh), and everyone else who graciously offered their help, I offer a million chords of thanks.

To my agent, Rachelle Gardner, who believed in this book before I even knew this book was a thing, thank you. Remember when I sent you that whiny email, lamenting the fact that I'd already rewritten certain chapters thirty times? Your reply was simple: "Go for thirty-one!" You push me to be and do my best. You fiercely fight for me. Thank you.

I also couldn't have done this without the support of various writing communities: thank you to the women of The Chapter for letting me post all the things, all the time, and for holding my tears when I didn't have a cup big enough to contain them. Thank you also to *She Loves Magazine* and *The Mudroom* for first giving me a space to work out my words, and to Jenny Rapson for inviting me to write the article that spawned this whole project. To those friends of the heart on the other side of Voxer, thank you for giving this lonely writer her necessary extrovert fill, and to Brenda Miller, thank you for graciously taking headshots of me and not making me feel too awkward in the process.

I'm eternally grateful for my beta readers, who took one look at the dastardly first draft and loved me all the same: Ashlee Thomas, Kurt Kroon, Micha Boyett, Alia Joy, and Lizzy Bailey, you hold rock star status in my book. Holly Hoeksema, Ruthie Johnson, Dorothy Greco, Courtney Ellis, Mindy Haidle, Lily Jensen, Heather Caliri, and Grace Hwang Lynch, thank you for reading smaller portions and offering invaluable insight. Ed Gilbreath and Quanny Ard, thank you for being a final set of eyes near the end of the project. Lisa Sharon Harper, Carolina Hinojosa-Cisneros, Kathy Khang, Idelette McVicker, and Osheta Moore, thank you for being brave enough to speak the truths that have changed me.

To the whole team at Zondervan: y'all are a powerhouse. Carolyn McCready, you are a gift. Thank you for your listening ear, your generous wisdom, and the myriad ways you pushed me to tell this story well. John Sloan, you are a brilliant editor who truly took the manuscript to the next level, but I've got to say: your brilliance really gave me a workout there! To Brandon Henderson, Brian Phipps, and the rest of the team, keep changing the world through the power of words. Thank you for believing in this project, sincerely.

To every friend, stranger-turned-friend, and family member who agreed to an interview, I'm so grateful you trusted me with your words and with your story: Dan MacDonald, Noel MacDonald, Brandon MacDonald, Aleah Dayton, Karen Driscoll, Meghan Driscoll, Kaitlin Jenkins, Kathy Higgins, Nat Higgins, James Howard Meredith, Insil Kang, Adrienne Davis, Kurt Kroon, Carl Paschual, Marlena Graves, Doug Jonson, CJ Peterson, Margo Starbuck, Riana Robinson, Josh McPaul, Jessica Ratliff, Shane Hopkins, Luke Atwood, Julie Akwabi-Ameyaw, Tim Fall, DeSean

Dyson, Teylar Greer, Tanya Fagan, Alicia Wassink, Tom Moody, Andrea Shetard, Alan (Toshimi) Itoh, Don Watson, Jamelyn Keatts, Rob Namba, J. Colin Petersen, Nicole Flowers, Lindsey Demary, Alyssa Robinowitz, Laura Siegel, and those who remain unnamed, thank you. Each of you is a part of this book.

To my parents, Dan and Noel, you are everything to me. Thank you for loving me even when we disagree and for trusting me to tell part of your story too. I honor the human in you. To James, Judy, and the entire Meredith family, thank you for embracing me and calling me your own.

To Canon and Theo, it is an honor to be your mama. How'd I ever get so lucky as to be able to tuck you in at night and slobber you with kisses and tickle-wrestle you on the floor of the living room? You've changed it all. And to James, the one my heart can't help but love, the one I'd say another million yeses to under a canopy of pines, thank you for being with me on this wild ride of life. I love you as much as you loved scrolling through your cell phone on our first date to find that perfect bottle of pinot noir. I choose you and I choose us and I choose our story, over and over again.

To God, the greatest redeemer and justice slinger of all, be the glory.

Notes

Chapter 3: Seeing Color for the First Time. Again.

1. In their book, *Nurture Shock* (New York: Twelve, 2009), authors Po Bronson and Ashley Merryman write that nonwhite parents are three times more likely to enter into conversations of race, while seventy-five percent of white parents never or almost never talk about race (52).

2. Erin Winkler, an associate professor of Africology at the University of Wisconsin-Milwaukee, cites a study that followed nearly two hundred children, ranging in age from six months to six years. Of the black and white participants, researchers found the youngest infants able to categorize people by race and gender ("Children Are Not Colorblind: How Young Children Learn Race," *Pace* 3, no. 3 (2009), *http://www. academia.edu/3094721/Children_Are_Not_Colorblind_How_Young_ Children_Learn_Race*). Bronson and Merryman state the same: shown a series of photographs of faces, babies will stare longer at a picture of someone of a different race, "trying to make sense of it. So faces that are familiar will actually get shorter visual attention" (Bronson and Merryman, *Nurture Shock*, 54).

Chapter 4: Well, I Love You

1. Amos 5:24 ESV.

2. Paraphrased from *America's Original Sin* (Grand Rapids, MI: Brazos, 2016) by Jim Wallis: An educational system "that allows white boys to assume success, yet leads black boys to cower from the institutions ostensibly created to protect everyone's well being" (13).

3. Acts 2:26 MSG.

4. David Crowder, quoted in "What Is the Difference between Compassion and Justice?" *Willow Creek Compassion and Justice Ministries,* September 28, 2009, *http://compassion.willowcreek.org/what-is -the-difference-between-compassion-and-justice/.*

5. Romans 16:16. And FYI, it's not about housing discrepancies.

6. In the early 1930s, President Roosevelt signed several housing-related acts, including the Home Owners' Loan Corporation (HOLC), aimed at helping individual home owners refinance their homes after the Great Depression, and the Federal Housing Authority (FHA), which sought to help provide homeowners' insurance (Ken Wytsma, *The Myth of Equality* [Downers Grove, IL: Intervarsity Press, 2017], 73). Before the HOLC closed in 1936, though, it partnered with the FHA to create "residential security maps," maps that outlined risk levels associated with certain properties. From this, realtors and lenders were able to decide which potential homebuyers *and* which particular houses most qualified for loans (74). "On the FHA/HOLC maps, neighborhoods outlined in green were marked with an *A* and described as areas that 'lacked a single foreigner or negro,' while neighborhoods with blacks living in them were given a *D* rating and made ineligible for FHA backing. *D* neighborhoods were outlined in red—and thus the term *redlining* was born," writes Ken Wytsma, author of *The Myth of Equality* (74). As segregation burgeoned across America, the real estate industry further ensured the establishment of ghettos in inner-city neighborhoods, as well as the negation of home ownership for potential black buyers, until Congress passed the Fair Housing Act of 1968. Although the new act prohibited discrimination and outlawed redlining based on race, color, religion, sex, and national origin or ancestry, it was too late (78). The damage had already been done. "Between 1983 and 2013," writes Wytsma, "home ownership rates among whites were roughly 25 percent higher than among nonwhites" (78). The evidence couldn't be denied.

7. Scott S. Smith, "James Meredith Smashed White Supremacy at Ole Miss," *Investor's Business Daily,* September 9, 2013, *https://www .investors.com/news/management/leaders-and-success/james-meredith -still-crusades-for-education-improvement/.*

8. United Methodist Church, "Racism and Economic Injustice against

People of Color in the US: 2016 Book of Resolutions, #3378," *https://www*
.umcjustice.org/who-we-are/social-principles-and-resolutions/racism-and
-economic-injustice-against-people-of-color-in-the-us-3378. Equally
interesting, the same article states that "despite steadily rising overall
wealth in the US, the 'wealth gap' between whites and African
Americans went from 12 to 1 in 1984 to 19 to 1 in 2009." The same was
true of net assets when "the median wealth of white families grew from
$46,000 in 1963 to $134,230 in 2013, while African American wealth
grew from $2,340 to $11,030" (Wytsma, *The Myth of Equality*), 78.

9. In a 2010 finding, "over 70% of the students involved in school-related
arrests or referred to law enforcement were Hispanic or Black," thus
making black students "three and a half times more likely to be
suspended or expelled than their white peers" (Thomas Rudd, "Racial
Disproportionality in School Discipline: Implicit Bias Is Heavily
Implicated," The Ohio State University Kirwan Institute for the Study
of Race and Ethnicity, February 5, 2015, *http://kirwaninstitute.osu.edu*
/racial-disproportionality-in-school-discipline-implicit-bias-is-heavily
-implicated/). The stories didn't stop there: in California, the state
James and I called home, blacks and Latinos were three times as likely
as whites to be stopped by the police, and in a 2010 study from the
Equal Justice Initiative, African Americans were illegally excluded
from criminal jury duty on a regular basis (Bill Quigley, "Fourteen
Examples of Systemic Racism in the US Criminal Justice System,"
Common Dreams, July 26, 2010, *https://www.commondreams.org/views*
/2010/07/26/fourteen-examples-systemic-racism-us-criminal-justice-system).
If there exists a greater chance of arrest as well as a lesser chance of
peer representation in the courtroom, it's no wonder that the "US
Bureau of Justice Statistics concludes that the chance of a black male
born in 2001 going to jail is 32% or 1 in three. Latino males have a
17% chance and white males have a 6% chance. Thus, black boys are
five times and Latino boys nearly three times as likely as white boys to
go to jail" (Quigley, "Fourteen Examples of Systemic Racism").

10. Civil rights lawyer, advocate and legal scholar Michelle Alexander
connects the two in *The New Jim Crow* (New York: The New Press,
2010) when she writes, "Parents and schoolteachers counsel black
children that, if they ever hope to escape this system and avoid prison
time, they must be on their best behavior, raise their arms and spread

their legs for the police without complaint, stay in failing schools, pull up their pants, and refuse all forms of illegal work and moneymaking activity, even if jobs in the legal economy are impossible to find" (215).

Chapter 5: Three Years in Mississippi

1. Let's just be honest here: in some places, even by force of habit, they still do.
2. Ann Bausum, *The March Against Fear* (Washington, DC: National Geographic, 2017), 9.
3. James Howard Meredith, *Three Years in Mississippi* (Bloomington, IN: Indiana Univ. Press, 1966), 5.
4. Meredith, *Three Years in Mississippi*, 50.
5. Meredith, *Three Years in Mississippi*, 54.
6. Meredith, *Three Years in Mississippi*, 57.
7. Luvvie Ajayi, *I'm Judging You* (New York: Holt Paperbacks, 2016), 86.
8. "James Meredith," *Wikipedia, https://en.wikipedia.org/wiki/James_Meredith*.
9. William Doyle's book, *An American Insurrection*, begins with this story. Powerful read!
10. A fine worth ten times that amount today.
11. "A Cross to Bear," *The Free Dictionary, http://idioms.thefreedictionary.com/a+cross+to+bear*.
12. I should mention that he wasn't the first man to attempt integration, but he was the first to successfully integrate and graduate. Look it up. Learn a little!
13. William Doyle, *An American Insurrection* (New York: Doubleday, 2001), 74.
14. Gen. 3:4–5.
15. Doyle, *An American Insurrection*, 159.
16. Doyle, *An American Insurrection*, 257.

Chapter 6: 1967, Then and Now

1. Rene Clausen, "Set Me as a Seal," *A New Creation,* Mark Foster/Shawnee Press, 1990. The text of the song comes from Song of Solomon 8:6–7.
2. With nods to the poem "Full Powers" by Pablo Neruda, in *Five Decades, a Selection (poems 1925–1970),* trans. Ben Belitt (New York: Grove, 1994), 265.

3. Sheryll Cashin, *Loving: Interracial Intimacy in America and the Threat to White Supremacy* (Boston: Beacon, 2017), 2.
4. By the time the Lovings said "I do," sixteen states, including their home state of Virginia, still prohibited interracial marriage. Oregon, my home state, repealed its miscegenation law banning marriages between whites and anyone who was one quarter or more black only seven years earlier. Likewise, as much as James and I touted the diversity in California, the state "still technically had a miscegenation law on its books in 1958, 'once the state Supreme Court declared the law invalid in the 1948 *Perez v. Sharp* case, it was no longer legally enforceable'" (Erin O'Neill, "Sheila Oliver Says 16 States Prohibited Interracial Marriage in 1958," *PolitiFact New Jersey,* January 15, 2012, *https://www.politifact.com/new-jersey/statements/2012/jan/15/sheila oliver /sheila-oliver-says-16-states-prohibited-interracial/*).
5. Hillary Kelly, "We Were Married on the Second Day of June, and the Police Came After Us the Fourteenth of July," *Washingtonian,* November 2, 2016, *https://www.washingtonian.com/2016/11/02/virginia case-legalized-interracial-marriage-the-loving-story/*.
6. Cashin, *Loving,* 110.
7. Cashin, *Loving,* 110. At that time, the judge also said these famous words, the logic of which the Supreme Court later disagreed with: "Almighty God created the races white, black, yellow, Malay and red, and he placed them on separate continents. And but for the interference with his arrangement there would be no cause for such marriages. The fact that he separated the races shows that he did not intend for the races to mix" ("Loving v. Virginia," *Cornell Law School: Legal Information Institute, https://www.law.cornell.edu/supremecourt /text/388/1*).
8. The Lovings had two young lawyers named Bernard Cohen and Philip Hirschkop.
9. Cashin, *Loving,* 105.
10. Here's what Chief Justice Warren said in the Supreme Court decision: "To deny this fundamental freedom on so unsupportable a basis as the racial classifications embodied in these statutes, classifications so directly subversive of the principle of equality at the heart of the Fourteenth Amendment, is surely to deprive all the State's citizens of liberty without due process of law" (Hillary Kelly, "We Were

Married on the Second Day of June, and the Police Came After Us the Fourteenth of July," Washingtonian, November 2, 2016, *https://www*
.washingtonian.com/2016/11/02/virginia-case-legalized-interracial-marriage
-the-loving-story/). Individual states no longer had the right to govern marriage, let alone decide the perceived thoughts and intentions of God.

Chapter 7: Differences

1. W. E. B. DuBois, quoted in Kyle D. Killian, *Interracial Couples, Intimacy and Therapy: Crossing Racial Borders* (New York: Columbia Univ. Press, 2013), 70.

2. "Commonality of oppression" came from a conversation on liberation theology from *The Liturgists Podcast.* (Mike McHargue, narrator, "Black and White: Racism in America," *The Liturgists Podcast,* episode 34, March 28, 2016, *http://www.theliturgists.com/podcast/2016/3 /29/episode-34-black-and-white-racism-in-america*).

3. E. Randolph Richards and Brandon J. O'Brien, *Misreading Scripture with Western Eyes: Removing Cultural Blinders to Better Understand the Bible* (Downers Grove, IL: Intervarsity, 2012), 54.

4. Killian, *Interracial Couples, Intimacy and Therapy,* 78.

5. This statistic is slightly higher than the national average of 17 percent who "in their first year of marriage in 2015 had crossed racial or ethnic lines," compared with a national average of 10 percent of all marriages, or around 11 million people (Jill Tucker, "As Intermarriage Spreads, Fault Lines Are Exposed," *San Francisco Chronicle,* May 19, 2017, *https://www.sfchronicle.com/nation/article/As-interracial-marriage -spreads-fault-lines-are-11157090.php*). Given that only 3 percent of marriages were interracial at the time Mildred and Richard Loving said their "I do's," such marriages increased tenfold by the end of the twentieth century. Between 2000 and 2010, interracial unions increased by an additional 28 percent (Killian, *Interracial Couples, Intimacy and Therapy,* 4). But choosing to cross racial borders in marriage comes with its own set of challenges, depending on geography, political inclination, age, and level of education.

"People who are younger, urban and college-educated are more likely to cross racial or ethnic lines on their trip to the altar, and those with liberal leanings are more apt to approve of the unions," writes Jill Tucker in an article for the *San Francisco Chronicle* ("As Intermarriage

Spreads, Fault Lines Are Exposed"). Citing results from a 2017 Pew Research survey in another article for the *San Francisco Gate*, Tucker writes, "49 percent of Democrats or those leaning Democrat said intermarriage was generally good for society, compared to 28 percent of Republicans or those leaning Republican" (Jill Tucker, "Big Disparities Found in Interracial Marriage—and Opinions on It," *SF Gate*, May 18, 2017, *https://www.sfgate.com/bayarea/article/Big-disparities-found-in-interracial-marriage-11155859.php*). Additionally, individuals who live in urban areas are more likely to marry outside of their race or ethnicity, with 18 percent of new marriages occurring between interracial couples living within city limits and 11 percent living outside of cities (Tucker, "Big Disparities Found in Interracial Marriage"). For instance, in San Francisco, where we lived, a city once known as the Harlem of the West, the black population fell from just more than 18 percent in the 1970s to less than 6 percent by the time James and I were married (Fred Jordan, "San Francisco Continues to Destroy Its Black Community," *Bay View National Black Newspaper*, April 15, 2016, *http://sfbayview.com/2016/04/san-francisco-continues-destroying-its-black-community/*). But the gentrification and forced out-migration of nearly 100,000 African Americans didn't decrease the number of intermarriages in the City by the Bay, because Asian and Hispanic communities continued to grow.

6. This is based on a comprehensive study from the Pew Research Center, cited in an article for the *San Francisco Chronicle* (Tucker, "As Intermarriage Spreads, Fault Lines Are Exposed").

7. Killian, *Interracial Couples, Intimacy and Therapy,* 2. Additionally, Killian cites a 2008 study that reports "29 percent of white respondents reject relationships of all types—dating, co-habitating, marrying and having children—with African Americans and Asian Americans" (2). And in a 2010 Pew Research study, "a full third of white respondents stated they would have a problem if a family member married a black person" (3).

8. Tucker, "Big Disparities Found in Interracial Marriage". In the same article she writes, "Among newlyweds, 24 percent of African American men are marrying someone of a different race or ethnicity, compared with 12 percent of black women." The number is significantly less among white newlyweds, the same study citing only 12 percent of white men and 10 percent of white women marrying

someone outside of their race or ethnicity, although this number
up from a notable 4 percent of white men and women marrying
outside of their race and ethnicity in 1980 (Gretchen Livingston and
Anna Brown, "Intermarriage in the U.S. Fifty Years after Loving v.
Virginia," *Pew Research Center,* May 18, 2017, *http://www.pewsocial
trends.org/2017/05/18/1-trends-and-patterns-in-intermarriage/*).

Chapter 8: Black Santa

1. Greg Nokes, "Black Exclusion Laws in Oregon," *The Oregon Encyclopedia,*
   updated March 17, 2018, *https://oregonencyclopedia.org/articles/exclusion
   _laws/#.WoHmgrbMyqD.*
2. Nokes, "Black Exclusion Laws in Oregon."
3. Oregon was admitted into the Union fifteen years later, on February 14,
   1859.
4. Five years later, Burnett became the first governor of California.
   Doesn't it make you wonder what influence Burnett had up and down
   the West Coast?
5. Nokes, "Black Exclusion Laws in Oregon."
6. Darrell Millner, "Blacks in Oregon," *The Oregon Encyclopedia,*
   updated June 29, 2018, *https://oregonencyclopedia.org/articles/blacks_in
   _oregon/#.WoHyK7bMw_W.*
7. Nokes, "Black Exclusion Laws in Oregon."
8. Nokes, "Black Exclusion Laws in Oregon."
9. Over a twenty-year period between the start and close of every exclusion
   act, there remained periods in which blacks *were* legally allowed to take
   up residency in the state. During these periods, African Americans
   established residency, and as new laws arose, those who were established
   remained exempt from the laws (Millner, "Blacks in Oregon").
10. From the final exclusion law, written into the state constitution: "No free
    negro or mulatto, not residing in this State at the time of the adoption
    of this constitution, shall ever come, reside, or be within this State,
    or hold any real estate, or make any contract, or maintain any
    suit therein; and the Legislative Assembly shall provide by penal
    laws for the removal by public officers of all such free negroes and
    mulattoes, and for their effectual exclusion from the State, and for
    the punishment of persons who shall bring them into the State, or
    employ or harbor them therein" (DeNeen L. Brown, "When Portland

Banned Blacks: Oregon's Shameful History as an 'All-White' State,"
Washington Post, June 7, 2017, *https://www.washingtonpost.com/news
/retropolis/wp/2017/06/07/when-portland-banned-blacks-oregons-shameful
-history-as-an-all-white-state/?utm_term=.de875fae1515).*

11. Brown, "When Portland Banned Blacks."

12. "US Constitution: Fourteenth Amendment," *Cornell Law School:
Legal Information Institute,* September 12, 2018, *https://www.law.cornell
.edu/constitution/amendmentxiv.*

13. Brown, "When Portland Banned Blacks."

14. Because of Oregon's racial homogeneity, conservatism, and gun culture,
"These attitudes were heartily embraced and very openly communicated by
white Oregonians. Storefronts throughout the state displayed signs reading,
'White Trade Only!' 'No Japs Allowed!' or 'No Dogs, No Indians!'
and worse" (Pete Kelley, "Why Is Bend So White? Understanding
Central Oregon's Racial History," *Vox Pop* 1 [summer 2017], 5).

15. D. L. Mayfield, "Facing Our Legacy of Lynching," *Christianity Today,*
August 18, 2017, *http://www.christianitytoday.com/ct/2017/september
/legacy-lynching-america-christians-repentance.html.*

16. Ps. 139:19.

Chapter 9: Learning to Listen

1. "Warner Sallman," *Wikipedia, https://en.wikipedia.org/wiki/Warner
_Sallman.*

2. See *https://www.metmuseum.org/art/collection/search/459087.*

3. Bob Duggan, "How Rembrandt Changed the Face of Jesus," *Big
Think,* n.d., *http://bigthink.com/Picture-This/how-rembrandt-changed-the
-face-of-jesus.*

4. "Why Do We Think Christ Was White?" *BBC,* March 27, 2001,
http://news.bbc.co.uk/2/hi/uk/1244037.stm.

5. "Why Do We Think Christ Was White?"

6. "Why Do We Think Christ Was White?"

7. Ta-Nehisi Coates, "What We Mean When We Say 'Race Is a Social
Construct,'" *Atlantic,* May 15, 2013, *https://www.theatlantic.com
/national/archive/2013/05/what-we-mean-when-we-say-race-is-a-social
-construct/275872/.*

8. Angela Onwuachi-Willig, "Race and Racial Identity Are Social
Constructs," *New York Times,* updated September 6, 2016, *https://www*

.nytimes.com/roomfordebate/2015/06/16/how-fluid-is-racial-identity/race-and-racial-identity-are-social-constructs.

9. Debby Irving, *Waking Up White* (Cambridge, MA: Elephant Room Press, 2014), location 735.

10. Irving, *Waking Up White,* 743.

11. Irving, *Waking Up White,* 750.

12. Aristotle Jones, "The Evolution: Slavery to Mass Incarceration," *Huffington Post,* October 6, 2016, *https://www.huffingtonpost.com/entry/the-evolution-slavery-to-mass-incarceration_us_57f66820e4b087a29a54880f.*

13. Michelle Alexander, *The New Jim Crow* (New York: The New Press, 2012), 7.

14. Lisa Sharon Harper, *The Very Good Gospel: How Everything Wrong Can Be Made Right* (Colorado Springs: Waterbrook, 2016), 20.

15. United States Census Bureau, "QuickFacts: San Mateo County, California," *https://www.census.gov/quickfacts/fact/table/sanmateocountycalifornia/PST045216.*

16. "Take up the White Man's burden / Send forth the best ye breed." In 1899, the first two lines of Rudyard Kipling's eight-stanza poem, "The White Man's Burden," helped "persuade anti-imperialist Americans to accept the annexation of the Philippine Islands to the United States." We were the only ones who could play savior to "Your new-caught, sullen peoples, / Half devil and half child," on the other side of the world, who most needed our help. "The White Man's Burden," *Wikipedia, https://en.wikipedia.org/wiki/The_White_Man%27s_Burden#cite_note-16.*

Chapter 10: Little Caramels

1. Part of this chapter first appeared as my article "Circle Only One," *She Loves Magazine,* March 26, 2017, *http://shelovesmagazine.com/2017/circle-only-one/.*

2. Lisa Sharon Harper, "The Very Good Gospel: Race, Dominion and the Image of God," *Auburn,* n.d., *https://auburnseminary.org/the-very-good-gospel-race-dominion-and-the-image-of-god/.*

3. Lisa Miller, "The Psychological Advantages of Strongly Identifying as Biracial," *The Cut,* May 22, 2015, *https://www.thecut.com/2015/05/psychological-advantages-biracial.html.*

4. "Multiracial in America," *Pew Research Center,* June 11, 2015, *http://www*

*.pewsocialtrends.org/2015/06/11/chapter-1-race-and-multiracial-americans
-in-the-u-s-census/*. This also pertains to the sentence that follows,
about the 1960 census.

5. D'Vera Cohn, "Seeking Better Data on Hispanics, Census Bureau
May Change How It Asks about Race," *Pew Research Center,* April 20,
2017, *http://www.pewresearch.org/fact-tank/2017/04/20/seeking-better-data
-on-hispanics-census-bureau-may-change-how-it-asks-about-race/*.

6. Jim Wallis, *America's Original Sin* (Grand Rapids, MI: Brazos, 2016), 2,
quoting Acts 17:26–27.

Chapter 11: *Imago Dei*

1. Brenda Salter McNeil, *Roadmap to Reconciliation* (Downers Grove, IL:
Intervarsity, 2015), 23.

2. McNeil, *Roadmap to Reconciliation*, 24.

3. Lisa Sharon Harper further proves this point when she writes, "The core
lie of Western civilization is that God reserved the power of dominion for
some, not all. Since the Enlightenment era, that lie has been radicalized.
With the founding of our nation, radicalized dominion was made law
with one resounding message: God reserved the right of dominion for
white people and no one else" (*The Very Good Gospel: How Everything
Wrong Can Be Made Right* [Colorado Springs: Waterbrook, 2016], 81).
Also, if as a white person you want to enact change, do not check the box
marked "white" in the 2020 census, but check the specifics of your ethnic
identity. Since 1790, there's been a single box marked "white" to check,
this single box only furthering dominance and supremacy in our country.

4. Maya Angelou said, "I come as one but I stand as ten thousand."

5. Cheryl Walker, ed., *American Women Poets of the Nineteenth Century:
An Anthology* (New Brunswick, NJ: Rutgers Univ. Press, 1995), 333.

6. John 4:13–14.

7. I believe I heard this interpretation of the sin of others in a sermon by
Dr. Brenda Salter McNeil.

8. I'll never forget the quote by Efrem Smith stated at a national Young
Life conference: "All lives matter equally to God. But in this upside-
down, broken, and bizarro world, not all lives are treated equally.
This is why we must say Black Lives Matter."

9. "Ubuntu Philosophy," *Wikipedia, https://en.wikipedia.org/wiki/Ubuntu
_philosophy*.

10. As I've learned, although the letter is often attributed to King alone, "A Letter from Birmingham Jail" was actually written by a number of individuals. If you haven't read it, cozy up and steady your hand to take notes. It's a must-read. See *https://www.africa.upenn.edu/Articles _Gen/Letter_Birmingham.html*.

11. Idelette McVicker, "How to Overwhelm the World," *Day 14: 28 Days of Inspiration for Dangerous Women,* 2018, *https://mailchi.mp/7eb14 efd0ad8/28-days-of-inspiration-2850705?e=defc6d12f9*.

12. Cara Meredith, "Goodbye HBH (the Moniker, That Is)," *CaraMeredith.com,* September 1, 2017, *http://carameredith.com/2017/09 /01/goodbye-hbh-moniker/*.

Chapter 12: The Problem

1. Paraphrasing Jurgen Moltmann: "Resistance is the protest of those who hope, and hope is the feast of the people who resist."

2. William Doyle, *An American Insurrection* (New York: Doubleday, 2001), 16–17.

3. "Jeremiah 5:21," *Pulpit Commentary,* BibleHub.com, *http://biblehub .com/commentaries/pulpit/jeremiah/5.htm*.

4. "Jeremiah 5:21," *Benson Commentary,* BibleHub.com, *http://biblehub .com/commentaries/benson/jeremiah/5.htm*.

5. James Howard Meredith, *Three Years in Mississippi* (Bloomington, IN: Indiana Univ. Press, 1966), 184.

6. Meredith, *Three Years in Mississippi,* 195–96. I love my father-in-law's account of the events that led up to the Ole Miss integration. While a number of books have been written on the subject, hearing him tell the story in his own words is pretty priceless. Also, the book is scheduled to rerelease in 2019.

7. Ann Bausum, *The March Against Fear* (Washington, D.C.: National Geographic, 2017), 7. Note: my father-in-law calls this the truest book ever written about him.

8. "40" by U2.

9. This trip took place in 2017. As of 2018, the Confederate flag is still being flown in parts of Mississippi, including the state capitol. In 2001, in a two-to-one margin, and again in 2015 in a four-to-one margin, Mississippi voters decided to keep the Confederate emblem as a part of the state flag. It is the only state whose flag still proudly boasts the archaic racist logo.

Chapter 13: Not Noticing

1. Jon Huckins and Jer Swigart, *Mending the Divides* (Downers Grove, IL: Intervarsity, 2017), 52.
2. Leah Donnella, "People of Color Accounted for 22 Percent of Children's Books Characters in 2016," *NPR,* February 17, 2017, *https://www.npr.org /sections/codeswitch/2017/02/17/515792141/authors-and-illustrators-of-color -accounted-for-22-percent-of-children-s-books.* This 2016 study examined children's books both written by people of color and featuring characters of color.
3. Jane Howard, "Doom and Glory of Knowing Who You Are," *Life* 54, no. 21 (May 24, 1963), 89.
4. "Privilege," *English Oxford Living Dictionaries,* 2018, *https://en.oxford dictionaries.com/definition/privilege.*
5. Christina Edmondson, dean of intercultural student development at Calvin College, quoted in Jemar Tisby, "The United States of Privilege," *Relevant* 91 (January/February 2018), 56–59.
6. Tisby, "The United States of Privilege." As Tisby points out, 46 percent of white people say they benefit from advantages that black people do not have, while 92 percent of black people say white people gain benefits because of their race. The numbers do not lie, even if for some of us the numbers remain hard to swallow.
7. Ken Wytsma, *The Myth of Equality* (Downers Grove, IL: Intervarsity, 2017), 26. Here's another thought to add: Many white people in America will never fully understand the advantages we have and the rights that have always been ours because an entire system has always been in our favor. But in this system of whiteness, whiteness isn't actually about the individual, but it's about an entire system of and structures infected by the disease and by the narrative.
8. The last five examples were all a part of Peggy McIntosh's concepts of white privilege from the essay "White Privilege and Male Privilege: A Personal Account of Coming to See Correspondences through Work in Women's Studies." Many historians say McIntosh, a women's studies scholar, coined the term when she began writing about it in the late eighties.
9. German Lopez, "Trump's Tweets about the NFL Protests Miss the Point Entirely," *Vox,* September 25, 2017, *https://www.vox.com/identities /2017/9/25/16361258/trump-nfl-protests-racism.*
10. Jon Schwarz, "Colin Kaepernick Is Righter Than You Know:

The National Anthem Is a Celebration of Slavery," *The Intercept,* August 28, 2016, *https://theintercept.com/2016/08/28/colin-kaepernick-is -righter-than-you-know-the-national-anthem-is-a-celebration-of-slavery/*.

11. Schwarz, "Colin Kaepernick Is Righter Than You Know."

12. Walter Olson, "Is 'The Star-Spangled Banner' Racist?" *National Review,* September 15, 2017, *http://www.nationalreview.com/article/451416/star -spangled-banner-racist-anthem*.

Chapter 14: A Beautiful Both-And

1. Hillary Kelly, "We Were Married on the Second Day of June, and the Police Came After Us the Fourteenth of July," *Washingtonian,* November 2, 2016, *https://www.washingtonian.com/2016/11/02/virginia -case-legalized-interracial-marriage-the-loving-story/*.

2. "Spawn," I should note, is the word naysayers used in various arguments I've read. This is not what I believe nor is it something I would call my children or any child.

3. "Rather than defend the racist logic animating the statute," the chief justice stated, "McIlawin [the state's attorney] tried to paint the state as concerned to protect the children of mixed marriages" (Sheryll Cashin, *Loving: Interracial Intimacy in America and the Threat to White Supremacy* [Boston: Beacon, 2017], 115). Virginia argued in favor of the Racial Integrity Act, a statute nothing less than racist in nature with its partiality toward maintaining a "pure white" race at the expense of black Virginian residents. Meanwhile, Philip Hirschkop and Bernard Cohen, the Loving's main attorneys, ignored the state's argument and focused instead on the Equal Protection Clause. The case wasn't about protecting the Loving's mixed-race children, he declared; it was about the state of Virginia upholding its racist laws.

4. *Help, Thanks, Wow: The Three Essential Prayers.* It's a book by Anne Lamott, one of my favorite authors.

5. Cara Meredith, "A Letter to My Black Son—With Love from Your White Mama," *For Every Mom,* January 17, 2016, *https://foreverymom .com/mom-gold/white-moms-letter-to-her-black-son/*.

6. Original quote from Austin Channing Brown on Jen Hatmaker's podcast: "I have no idea what you should do, but you should do something. You can do something and it's your job to figure out what that something is and to let that something lead to more and more somethings" ("For the

Love of Exploring Our Faith Episode 04: Knowing Where We've Been to Get Where We're Going: Austin Channing Brown," *Jenhatmaker. com, http://jenhatmaker.com/episode-04-austin-channing-brown*). Also, y'all, if you haven't picked up Austin's book, *I'm Still Here,* stop staring at the endnotes, put my book down, and start reading hers immediately.

7. Bowbay Feng and Miriam Lundy, "On the Experience of Being Mixed: A Juxtaposition of Pride and Shame," presentation, California Association of Marriage and Family Therapists, April 2015.

8. Jamie Frayer, "My Daughter Is Diluted," in *Being Biracial: Where Our Secret Worlds Collide,* ed. Sarah Ratliff and Bryony Sutherland (Utuado, Puerto Rico: Coqui Press, 2015), location 940.

9. Frayer, *Being Biracial,* location 962.

10. "Mixed Races," *Racial Slur Database,* September 15, 2018, *http://rsdb .org/races#mixed_races.*

11. Jason Kashdan, "Want Smarter Kids? Genetic Diversity Could Be Key," *CBS News,* July 2, 2015, *https://www.cbsnews.com/news/new-study -finds-genetic-diversity-may-be-key-taller-smarter/.*

12. Janek O'Toole, "On Being Everyone and No One," in *Being Biracial: Where Our Secret Worlds Collide,* ed. Sarah Ratliff and Bryony Sutherland (Utuado, Puerto Rico: Coqui Press, 2015), location 1047.

13. Souad Yasmine, "Born from a Paradox," in *Being Biracial: Where Our Secret Worlds Collide,* ed. Sarah Ratliff and Bryony Sutherland (Utuado, Puerto Rico: Coqui Press, 2015), location 1554.

14. Shane Hopkins, Skype interview by the author, September 9, 2016.

15. Teylar Greer, interview by the author in person, July 2017.

16. Rev. 22:1–5.

17. "Minorities Expected to Be Majority in 2050," *CNN,* August 13, 2008, *http://www.cnn.com/2008/US/08/13/census.minorities/.* The article also states that the number of US residents who identify as mixed-race is projected to triple, from 5.2 million to 16.2 million.

18. "Minorities Expected to Be Majority in 2050." Also, some predictions decrease statistics by a couple of years, with minority children surpassing the 50 percent mark by 2020. Likewise, those who identify as mixed-race will experience a whopping growth of 225.5 percent increase, from 2.5 percent of the US population in 2014 to 6.2 percent of the population in 2060.

19. Lisa Sharon Harper, *The Very Good Gospel: How Everything Wrong Can Be Made Right* (Colorado Springs: Waterbrook, 2016), 12.

20. Walter Brueggemann, *Living Toward a Vision: Biblical Reflections on Shalom* (New York: United Church Press, 1984), 15.
21. Osheta Moore, *Shalom Sistas* (Harrisonburg, VA: Herald, 2017), 30.
22. Rob Bell, *Velvet Elvis: Repainting the Christian Faith* (San Francisco: Harper One, 2012), 107.

Chapter 15: We, Ours, Us

1. Julie Akwabi-Ameyaw, conversation with the author, October 2016.
2. Ashley Fantz, Steve Almasy, and Catherine E. Shoichet, "Tamir Rice Shooting: No Charges for Officers," *CNN,* December 28, 2015, *http://www.cnn.com/2015/12/28/us/tamir-rice-shooting/index.html*.
3. Christine Mai-Duc, "Cleveland Officer Who Killed Tamir Rice Had Been Deemed Unfit for Duty," *Los Angeles Times,* December 3, 2014, *http://beta.latimes.com/nation/nationnow/la-na-nn-cleveland-tamir-rice -timothy-loehmann-20141203-story.html*.
4. Adrienne Davis, Skype interview by the author, June 2016.
5. "New Faces of American Babies" (video clip), *ABC News,* n.d., *http://abc news.go.com/WNT/video/gerber-baby-food-children-kids-moms-family -parenting-13935466*. I should add that it is a delight to see Gerber feature a child born with Down syndrome as the 2018 Gerber Baby. Bravo. This matters. This counts.
6. Ruby Sales, "Where Does It Hurt?" interview by Krista Tippett, *On Being,* September 15, 2016, *https://onbeing.org/programs/ruby-sales-where -does-it-hurt/*.
7. "Ruby Sales," *Wikipedia, https://en.wikipedia.org/wiki/Ruby_Sales*.
8. "About the Founder and Director," *The SpiritHouse Project, http://www .spirithouseproject.org/aboutruby.php*.
9. Author's notes from that night.
10. Author's notes. I've also heard this from numerous other people. Technically, even if we don't have Jim Crow laws on the books, we definitely still have Jim Crow hate.
11. Author's notes.
12. Sales, "Where Does It Hurt?"

Chapter 16: Lamentations

1. The Declaration of Independence, y'all.
2. "The Paradox of Liberty" was on a sign at the entrance to that scene.

3. Sarah Shin, *Beyond Colorblind: Redeeming Our Ethnic Journey* (Downers Grove, IL: Intervarsity, 2017), 160.
4. "This Day in History: August 28, 1955, Emmett Till Is Murdered," *History, www.history.com/this-day-in-history/the-death-of-emmett-till.*
5. "Mamie Till," *Wikipedia, https://en.wikipedia.org/wiki/Mamie_Till.*
6. John W. Fountain, "Mamie Mobley, 81, Dies; Son, Emmett Till, Slain in 1955," *New York Times,* January 7, 2003, *www.nytimes.com/2003 /01/07/us/mamie-mobley-81-dies-son-emmett-till-slain-in-1955.html.*
7. *The Body of Emmett Till: The Story behind David Jackson's Photograph,* directors Kira Pollack and Paul Moakley, Red Border Films/*Time,* short documentary film, in the *Time* series 100 Photographs: The Most Influential Images of All Time, n.d., *http://100photos.time.com /photos/emmett-till-david-jackson.*
8. *The Body of Emmett Till.*
9. Shannon Dingle, "Maybe White Pushback against the African American History Museum Is about Something More," *ShannonDingle.com,* September 26, 2016, *http://www.shannondingle.com/blog//maybe-white-push back-against-the-african-american-history-museum-is-about-something-more.*
10. Daniel Hill, *White Awake* (Downers Grove, IL: Intervarsity, 2017), 106.
11. Rom. 12:15.
12. Soong-Chan Rah, *Prophetic Lament* (Downers Grove, IL: Intervarsity, 2015), 46. I've also thought a lot about this quote from Dr. Rah: "Lamentations incorporates a myriad of voices to strengthen the narrative of the suffering of God's people. The vast array of voices reflected in Lamentations deepens our appreciation of the lament over fallen Jerusalem. The power of Lamentations is that the voices of those who have actually suffered are not missing" (103).

Chapter 17: Tramp, Tramp, Tramping of Feet

1. Ann Bausum, *The March Against Fear* (Washington, D.C.: National Geographic, 2017), 14.
2. Bausum, *The March Against Fear,* 14.
3. Norvell was sentenced to two years in prison for his crime but was released after eighteen months.
4. "Pulitzer Prize Photograph of the Year: 1967," *Bytes,* November 2, 2013, *http://bytesdaily.blogspot.com/2013/11/pulitzer-photograph-of-year -1967.html.*

5. Bausum, *The March Against Fear,* 6.

6. Bausum, *The March Against Fear,* 7.

7. "The Big Five" in order of arrival: King of the SCLC, Floyd McKissick of CORE (Congress of Racial Equality), Carmichael of SNCC, Whitney Young of the National Urban League, and Roy Wilkins of the NAACP (National Association for the Advancement of Colored People) [Bausum, *The March Against Fear,* 24].

8. Luke 10:33–35.

9. Bausum, *The March Against Fear,* 31.

10. Bausum, *The March Against Fear,* 1.

11. Bausum, *The March Against Fear,* 75.

12. Bausum, *The March Against Fear,* 81.

13. Jamil Smith, "The Revolutionary Power of *Black Panther:* Marvel's New Movie Marks a Major Milestone," *Time,* n.d., *http://time.com /black-panther/.*

14. Smith, "The Revolutionary Power of *Black Panther.*"

15. Bausum, *The March Against Fear,* 81.

16. "The moral arc of the universe is long, but it bends toward justice" (Martin Luther King Jr., "'A Look to the Future,' Address Delivered at Highlander Folk School's Twenty-fifth Anniversary Meeting," *Stanford: The Martin Luther King, Jr. Research and Education Institute,* September 2, 1957, *https://kinginstitute.stanford.edu/king-papers/docu ments/look-future-address-delivered-highlander-folk-schools-twenty-fifth -anniversary*).

17. Just so we're clear, I am *not* ending this book with an "All Lives Matter" proclamation, because until we don't have to say it anymore, Black Lives Matter.

Recommended Reading

Want to read more? Start here.

Exploring Race and Justice in America

Just Mercy (Bryan Stevenson)

The New Jim Crow (Michelle Alexander)

The Warmth of Other Suns (Isabel Wilkerson)

We Were Eight Years in Power (Ta-Nehisi Coates)

Working toward Justice and Healing in the Church

Roadmap to Reconciliation (Brenda Salter McNeil)

The Very Good Gospel (Lisa Sharon Harper)

Prophetic Lament (Soong-Chan Rah)

Beyond Colorblind (Sarah Shin)

Embracing New Narratives of History

Go Tell it on the Mountain (James Baldwin)

Strength to Love (Martin Luther King Jr.)

An American Insurrection (William Doyle)

The March Against Fear (Ann Bausum)

Understanding the Privilege of Whiteness

White Awake (Daniel Hill)
The Myth of Equality (Ken Wytsma)
Waking Up White (Debby Irving)
What Does It Mean to Be White? (Robin DiAngelo)